Living without a Why

Living without a Why

MYSTICISM, PLURALISM, AND THE WAY OF GRACE

Paul O. Ingram

Foreword by Marit Trelstad

CASCADE *Books* • Eugene, Oregon

LIVING WITHOUT A WHY
Mysticism, Pluralism, and the Way of Grace

Copyright © 2014 Paul O. Ingram. All rights reserved. Except for brief quotations in critical publications or reviews, no part of this book may be reproduced in any manner without prior written permission from the publisher. Write: Permissions, Wipf and Stock Publishers, 199 W. 8th Ave., Suite 3, Eugene, OR 97401.

Cascade Books
An Imprint of Wipf and Stock Publishers
199 W. 8th Ave., Suite 3
Eugene, OR 97401

www.wipfandstock.com

ISBN 13: 978-1-62564-707-8

Cataloging-in-Publication data:

Ingram, Paul O., 1939–

Living without a why : mysticism, pluralism, and the way of grace / Paul O. Ingram, with a foreword by Marit Trelstad.

xii +124 p. 23 cm—Bibliographical references and indexes.

ISBN 13: 978-1-62564-707-8

1. Porete, Marguerite, approximately 1250–1310. 2. Christianity and other religions—Buddhism. 3. Mysticism—History—Middle Ages, 600–1500. 4. Buddhism—Relations—Christianity. 5. Spirituality—Lutheran Church. I. Trelstad, Marit, 1967–. II. Title.

BV5075 I54 2014

Scripture references are taken from the New Revised Standard Version Bible, copyright 1989 by the National Council of the Churches of Christ in the United States of America. Used by permission. All rights reserved.

Manufactured in the USA

Contents

Foreword by Marit Trelstad | vii

Preface | xi

1. Introduction | 1
2. History of Religions: Methodology as Metaphor | 11
3. The Difficult Path | 29
4. What's in a Name? | 47
5. Butterfly in a Mirror | 57
6. A Theological Reflection on Mystical Experience | 75
7. The Jesus Way of Living without a Why | 89
8. Living without a Why: The Way of Grace | 109

Bibliography | 117
Scripture Index | 121
Index of Names | 123

Foreword

MANY YEARS AGO, AT a 1993 conference titled Reimagining: A Global Theological Conference by Women, theologian Chung Hyun Kyung delivered a thrilling lecture about breaking taboos. Taboos, she argued, are boundaries set by authorities that often simply protect the power of the privileged. Therefore, we need to question and push at boundaries restricting access, knowledge, and truth that may liberate. On the podium was a big red apple to symbolize the fall in the garden of Eden—the first taboo restricting knowledge in the Bible—and, to the delight of her audience, she took a big bite from it before continuing her lecture.

In this book, *Living Without a Why*, Paul Ingram also demonstrates an interest in transgressing boundaries—both academic and religious—in a mature search for truth. This work is in concert with his most recent publications that demonstrate his interests in Whiteheadian process theology, Buddhist-Christian dialogue, and the science-religion dialogue. His most recent books are *Wrestling with the Ox* (Wipf & Stock, 2006), *Wrestling with God* (Cascade Books, 2006), *Buddhist-Christian Dialogue in an Age of Science* (Rowman & Littlefield, 2007), *The Process of Buddhist-Christian Dialogue* (Cascade Books, 2009), *Theological Reflections at the Boundaries* (Cascade Books, 2011), and *Passing Over and Returning: A Pluralist Theology of Religions* (Cascade Books, 2013). In *Living without a Why*, he engages a wide variety of fields and methods of scholarship such as history of religions, and theology and science, but he seeks, in each chapter, to unite objective scholarship to the intimately personal and subjective knowing that comes through mysticism and religious or personal experience.

In the opening chapters, he argues for a unity of the subjective and objective forms of knowing, an epistemology that does not engage a false (though prevalent) idea that the knower and the known can be separated. He utilizes Whitehead's process philosophy and theology to describe an interrelated reality where these separations are foundationally challenged.

FOREWORD

As most of us in the academic field of religion can attest, we live at a time when religious experience is often observed and studied as though it can be separated out from any truth claims of believers themselves. We have bought the scientist assumption that truth, reliability, and objectivity are linked or, worse, that data is truth. Thus, we cannot engage subjective experience as a medium of truth—even when we are studying religion. Ingram argues that this presumed objectivity flattens the very richness of religion and employs false boundaries that block truth itself. Ingram asks that we employ the best of all fields—science, history, religious experience—and methods in a coherent search for knowledge.

Thus, in later chapters, one finds Ingram uniting the methods of his original field—history of religions—with religious experience and theological claims of believers. Also, he explores how mysticism and science, Buddhist and Christian scholars, can cross-pollinate and overlap in ways that lead us further on a path of truth. But, to use the words of Pilate in the Gospel of John, what is truth? When Ingram uses the word *truth*, he is not describing a universal, unchanging, static reality, but rather an ever-developing path on which we are led—it is the Way. This Way is described by famous Buddhist thinkers as well as by Christian mystics and theologians, whom Ingram brings richly together. He deeply engages Christian mystic Marguarite Porete, the Daoist sage Zuangzi, and Martin Luther. In a separate chapter, he embraces the understanding of Jesus as Jewish mystic and political revolutionary who is able to transgress religious and social boundaries, to lead his followers to new, risky forms of living and truth. Along all these lines of inquiry, Ingram finds cross-paths and clues to lead readers to understand the paradox of where knowledge and letting-go-of-knowledge meet in religious experience of truth. Living without a why is the peace that comes from engaging both sides of the paradox fully.

How do we know we are on the path of truth and not delusion? There are three main pointers that emerge over the course of the book. First, in several places in the book, Ingram offers a Buddhist-Christian view that the fruits of the Way are ultimately liberating. When one seeks to define, exclude and control other people or the truth itself, one knows that one is off track. Second, Ingram offers that when we cling to our methods and doctrines and symbols, refusing all others, this is a symptom of fear, and it will lead us to illusion. When we let go of knowing, while simultaneously engaging many ways of knowledge, we will get closer to our objective. Third, Ingram points to Jesus as model of living the Way. Beyond Jesus, however, he points to examples throughout Buddhist and Christian history of leaders who were able to reach across the aisle to other traditions and norms—to lead to deeper ways of living. Implicit in Ingram's book is the notion that conventional truths and ways of living or relating are often misleading since they point more to culture than to sacred reality.

We can point to the truth or the Sacred with our language, symbols, and ritual, but we cannot own or possess it. While Christian theology has long claimed that God is incomprehensible mystery, Ingram also adds that "the Sacred—however named—is the Ultimate Mystery and ineffable boundary generating the cognitive dissonance inherent in all theological reflection. All religious Ways reflect the Sacred according to their own distinctive ways. But none can own the Sacred or claim absolute truth about the Sacred. The Sacred, however named, is not only ineffable but also radically pluralistic"[1] The Sacred and reality itself is ultimately unknowable but intimately experienced in multiple forms. Thus, Ingram (in a very Lutheran manner) urges religious practitioners to place our trust in the grace that surrounds us and then to let go of reins and live.

In an age of contextual religious studies, Ingram's description of the Sacred is refreshingly universal while still affirming pluralism. While he addresses this in other works, I would offer that Ingram could spend more time discussing how truth or a path of living can be liberating in one context but in another oppressive. As a feminist theologian, I also find that mysticism has certain patriarchal traps—affirming detachment (at least initially) as necessary, rather than full relational engagement. Also, mysticism requires a certain level of luxury or privilege that is difficult to access when one is a full-time caregiver of others. The founder of the Social Gospel movement, Walter Rauschenbusch, wrote how mysticism is important, but it cannot lead away from social engagement. And Ingram agrees heartily with this throughout the book, and offers interesting insight from both Christianity and Buddhism as to how mysticism can lead to social engagement.

No doubt readers will find Ingram's counteracademic moves of reengaging the subjective, the nondata, and the mystical to be refreshing as he affirms these in ways that do not contradict but embrace all forms of knowing. At this particular time in the academic study of religion, it is a very necessary move away from the form of religious study that has been overly shaped by the methods of science and by the insistence that observation alone leads to truth. The empirical method is excellent for some forms of

---

1. See pages 53–54.

FOREWORD

science, but it has reigned supreme and taken over other areas of study in a way that is unwarranted. And, on a personal level, I find the beauty of Ingram's writing and insights to always help me see the Sacred in and between the world religions and human experience in its manifold manifestations. I also cannot help but delight in and affirm the pushing of boundaries between the disciplines and methods that Ingram employs. Dear readers, enjoy!

Marit Trelstad

Preface

I HAVE BEEN FASCINATED by Christian mysticism, sometimes called negative theology, since my first encounter with Marguerite Porete's *Mirror of Simple Souls* during my undergraduate days. The *Mirror* not only provided me with an opening to other Christian mystical writers, but it also opened me to the writings of mystics who populate, beyond counting, non-Christian traditions. Porete's mystical theology still inspires me and is the inspiration for each chapter in this book, particularly her notion of "living without a why," which she defined as life lived in union with God's will. "Living without a why" was also her description of the life of grace and, when all is said and done, I think is quite similar to Martin Luther's theology of grace.[1] Accordingly each chapter in this book comprises theological reflections from a Lutheran historian of religions on the life of grace inspired by Marguerite Porete's mirror. More is known about Martin Luther than about Marguerite Porete; what we know of Porete is that she was a French beguine mystic who wrote a single text, *The Mirror of Simple Souls*, for which she was burned at the stake for heresy in Paris in 1310. She was in all probability a solitary beguine who might have been an itinerant teacher to interested listeners. She wrote the *Mirror* in Old French sometime between 1296 and 1306, and some of her ideas were appropriated by Meister Eckhart, and through Eckhart, may have influenced Martin Luther during his tenure as an Augustinian friar.

The solitude of a writer is never absolute. We depend on others, especially on those whose expertise is a source for shaping one's ideas. In particular, I am deeply grateful to Douglas A. Oakman, who has read chapter 7 and offered both support and valuable criticism. Doug is one of the leading New Testament scholars in North America. He specializes in historical Jesus research with a focus on the peasant context of Jesus's life in first-century Galilee and his depiction of Jesus as a political activist. He

1. Hamm, *The Early Luther*, chap. 8.

PREFACE

has also published brilliant work on Saint Paul's Christology.[2] We have been colleagues and friends for twenty-five years as members of the Department of Religion at Pacific Lutheran University, and I deeply appreciate his critical support of my work.

I am also grateful to Dr. Marit Trelstad for contributing the Foreword to this volume. She currently serves as chair of the Department of Religion at Pacific Lutheran University and is one of the more creative Lutheran feminist theologians working in North America. Her work and mine are deeply influenced by the process vision of reality of Alfred North Whitehead, whose work we both encountered as students of John B. Cobb Jr. during our days as graduate students at the Claremont Graduate University—although I preceded her by more years than I like to remember. We are two of a rather small number of Lutherans who have incorporated process thought into our particular theological reflections.

I also want to thank K. C. Hanson, editor-in-chief at Cascade Books for bringing yet another of my manuscripts to publication. I am also grateful to two of his colleagues at Cascade Books for their careful editorial assistance: Jeremy Funk and Heather Carraher. It is a pleasure beyond measure to work with such skilled professionals.

This book is dedicated to John B. Cobb Jr. About six years ago my wife, Regina, and I were visiting with John and his wife, Jean, in Claremont. During a conversation in his living room after lunch, he asked me about my future plans for publication. At the time, I was, and still am, heavily focused on Buddhist–Christian dialogue and science–religion dialogue. But I approached these topics as a historian of religions rather than as a theologian—or so I thought. At the end of our conversation, John smiled and said, "Paul, you're a theologian."

"I thought I was a historian of religions," I said. "No one's ever called me a 'theologian' before. What do you mean?"

"Just think about it and you'll come to your own conclusions," he answered."

I have been thinking about it ever since. In fact, it has been my *koan* for the last six years. This book along with my earlier volumes, *Theological Reflections at the Boundaries* and *Passing Over and Returning: A Pluralist Theology of Religions*, represent how I am still thinking about it. For initiating me into an unexpected, and at the time undesired, theological journey of creative transformation, my gratitude to John Cobb is beyond measure.

2. Most notably, see Oakman, "The Perennial Relevance of Saint Paul."

ONE

Introduction

ON NOVEMBER 8, 2000, I preached a sermon titled "The Epiphany of Jesus" at a morning chapel service at Pacific Lutheran University in Tacoma, Washington.[1] My chosen text for that morning was Mark 9:33–40. Since the topic of each chapter in this book is inspired by my theological reflection on these verses in Mark's gospel contextualized by my reading of Marguerite Porete's *Mirror of Simple Souls*, I thought it best to include this sermon as my beginning point. I have broken Mark's text into two sets of verses for reasons I hope will be clear. First, Mark 9:33–37:

> And they came to Capernaum; and when he was in the house he asked them, "What were you discussing on the way?" But they were silent; for on the way they had discussed with one another who was the greatest. And he sat down and called the twelve; and he said to them, "If any one would be first, he must be last of all and servant of all." And he took a child, and put him in the midst of them; and taking him in his arms, he said to them," Whoever receives one such child in my name receives me; and whoever receives me, receives not me, but him who sent me.

Jesus's question to Peter—"Who do you say that I am?"—is the heart of Christian self-understanding and must be answered differently in every age. We do not live in the first century or the Middle Ages or the nineteenth century. Clinging to past images of Jesus and his relation to God simply will not do in our contemporary, global context of religious and cultural pluralism. This is not surprising, since Christians have been practicing faith within globally pluralistic contexts for two thousand years.

1. This sermon is a slight revision of the sermon in Ingram, *Wrestling with God*, 20–25.

We still haven't got it right, even though the answer to Jesus's question to Peter is right in front of us, as it was for the disciples: stalking us like a cougar after prey. According to Mark's gospel, the disciples didn't get it right either, even though they followed Jesus around Palestine for perhaps a year. Jesus tried to tell them, yet even they didn't see the answer staring them in the face until after Jesus was killed, and even then only vaguely.

In Mark's text, Jesus and the disciples have returned to his home in Capernaum after an extended journey. On the way to Caesarea Philippi Jesus had questioned the disciples about his identity. Now on the way back home, the disciples are arguing about their own self-images. When Jesus questions them again, they fall silent with embarrassment because they have been arguing about the preeminence of self—over who is the greatest. They are like fundamentalists everywhere in all times and in all places in all religious traditions: trapped in the conventional categories of their religious systems. They, like Jesus, are practicing Jews. But unlike Jesus, they cling to their culture's conventional Judaism so tightly they can't hear the music behind the lyrics of either Jewish practices or Jesus's teachings. Like legalists and fundamentalists of all ages in all religious traditions, their path is one of fabricating verbal argumentation, of imaging a self—or a particular community of selves—exalted above others at the center of their conventional world. Their journey with Jesus has not awakened them. Instead, they see Jesus as their ticket to glory, to permanent selfhood exalted.

So once more Jesus instructs them about discipleship. His teaching method is to consistently subvert their notions of discipleship as a preeminence of position. "He who would be first must be last," he says. To make one's self last means negating the absolute nature of one's self, of one's *persona*. This is why receiving Jesus and the one who sent him in Mark and elsewhere in other gospel texts is exemplified as the receiving of a little child—of one who has not yet developed a strong self-image, of one who has no rank or importance beyond their particular families. It is Jesus who approaches the disciples and the readers of Mark as a child, with no rank or importance whatsoever. It is God who sent Jesus, who approaches the disciples and us as a child, not as the romanticized image of sweet innocence, but the weakest of the weak.

Our first response as readers of Mark's text is to disassociate ourselves from the egotistical disciples. In previous verses Jesus had just been speaking about the inevitability of his suffering and dying. And the disciples' insensitivity to Jesus's fate, combined with their crass egoism, is not a stance a reader is likely to willingly embrace. But by a rhetorical sleight of hand, the Markan Jesus directly addresses the reader—meaning us—through a series of paradoxical "if" and "whoever" statements: "If anyone would be first, he must be last of all and servant of all"; "Whoever receives one such child in my name receives me"; "whoever receives me, receives not me but him who sent me."

The experience of paradox is the experience of being bracketed between seemingly incompatible but nevertheless coexisting pairs of opposites. Even Mark's language about God is paradoxical. Who is the "who" that sent Jesus? Why does Mark not explicitly identify God as Jesus's sender? The Markan Jesus simply says that to receive the weakest of the weak is to receive him and "him who sent me." In the same way, the voice of God speaks from the heavens at Jesus's baptism in chapter 1, verse 1, and again from a cloud at Jesus's transfiguration. Yet Mark fails to mention just whose voice is speaking. And again, when the Markan Jesus addresses his Father in Gethsemane, in response no voice is heard at all. But Jesus is portrayed as the Son of God and our assumption that the voices Mark allows us to hear are from God is not mistaken. What *is* mistaken is that we know what this means. Not only is Jesus impossible to identify in clear definitions, God is too. What, then, could it mean to be great?

Now Mark 9:38–40:

> John said to him, "Teacher, we saw a man casting out demons in your name, and we forbade him, because he was not following us." But Jesus said, "Do not forbid him; for no one who does a mighty work in my name will be able soon after to speak evil of me. For he who is not against us is for us."

Now the disciple John changes the question by latching onto the name of Jesus to bring up the issue of just who can be said to belong to the Jesus movement. After all, throughout Mark's gospel, Jesus harshly criticizes various groups of people—the Pharisees, the scribes, the Jerusalem temple priests. Who could blame John for concluding that the disciples constitute a well-defined, exclusive group over against outsiders? Indeed, defining a social identity was an important issue for the early church, as it still is today. But party spirit does not come from receiving Jesus and God as one would receive a child, but from a conventionally fearful mind that draws artificial boundaries around people as a religious prophylaxis to protect one's community from coming into contact with whatever one regards as threatening. These very boundaries Jesus has been at pains to undermine.

Jesus does not recommend party identity, but opens up community to anyone who is not against him. There are no fixed criteria for membership in the Jesus community—beyond the requirement that one not be against it. There is no imagined pattern of Christian self-identity, no gold card of membership. Jesus's teachings in Mark are pluralist, not exclusivist: they apply to all who are not against Jesus, not only Christians, but also non-Christians: Buddhists who revere Jesus as an awakened person (that is, a Bodhisattva); Muslims, who revere Jesus as one of the greatest prophets; Jews, who see Jesus as a reformer calling people to a renewed practice of the Torah.

Of course, these non-Christians do not accept Christian *ideas* about Jesus. Yet Jesus's teaching recorded here in Mark makes no such stipulation. To be *for* Jesus does not necessarily mean accepting ideas *about* Jesus. Ideas about Jesus—creeds, doctrines, theological constructions in general—flow out of conventional wisdom and are tied to historical and cultural contexts and are empty of unchanging essence and once-and-for-all timeless meanings. Note that Mark himself gives no clear definitions, because the author of Mark is the first deconstructionist of the Jesus movement. His Jesus and the God who sent Jesus shy away from self-definition. The messiah is not the glory figure of the disciples' conventional expectations, but one who experiences the sufferings, sorrows, and joys of a lived life. The follower of Jesus is not one who belongs to the proper group. Anyone who is not against Jesus is a follower of Jesus; this makes for a very pluralistic community indeed.

So what does Mark teach us about following the way of Jesus two thousand years after the disciples tried and failed? I think Mark teaches us negative and positive lessons. Negatively, Mark's deconstructs human pretensions about who is greatest, along with claims that any single group of followers of Jesus has an exclusive claim on truth *about* Jesus and the one who sent Jesus. Mark's deconstruction tells us that Christian faith is not about ripping biblical texts out of context as a means of proving who's really Christian and who's not. Mark teaches us that no human being and no religious community is greater than another human being or religious community. Mark teaches us that God doesn't give a damn about religion, but cares very much about human beings and the rest of creation. Mark teaches us that faith is not adherence to a set of doctrinal propositions about Jesus and the one who sent Jesus. Mark teaches us that Jesus and the one who sent him cannot be contained by ritual and theological systems.

INTRODUCTION

Mark teaches us that clinging to conventional practices and conventional understandings that try to lock God within the safe boundaries of our cultural expectations while excluding those who do not see things our way is not faith but unfaith. Mark teaches us that we should never transform faith into a set of ideological propositions. We should never confuse theological reflection, which Saint Anslem called "faith seeking understanding," with ideology.

Positively, Mark teaches us that we find Jesus and the one who sent Jesus incarnated in the ordinary; in loving relationships between people; in the struggle against economic, political, gender and racial injustice; in the struggle for ecological justice that frees nature—God's creation—from human exploitation. We meet Jesus and the one who sent Jesus wherever and whenever persons work for justice. Following the way of Jesus is not a matter of membership in a particular Christian group or of wearing a particular Christian label like *Lutheran* or *Roman Catholic* or *Presbyterian* or *Baptist*. The Jesus community that Mark envisioned includes anyone who is not against Jesus: the socially engaged Buddhist layman Sulak Sivaraksa, who has time and again placed his life in danger for his criticism of the Thai government's financial involvement in the drug trade and sex trade of his country; Dr. Cecil Murray, retired senior pastor of the First AME Church in Los Angeles, whose educational vision and social outreach to the poor and homeless has become a model for similar social programs throughout the counties of Southern California; Mahatma Gandhi, who followed the principle of nonviolence in his struggle to free his people from British colonialism; Gandhi's Muslim friend Badhsha Khan, who transformed the Qur'an's teaching of *jihad* or "struggle" into nonviolent resistance against the injustices of British colonialism; Martin Luther King Jr., who apprehended Jesus and the one who sent Jesus in his fight against American racism. All of these are followers of Jesus, as are each of us, when we feed the poor; when we refuse to oppress people because of gender, ethnicity, or race; when we do not confuse membership in the Jesus community with membership in any particular form of the institutional church. We are followers of Jesus and the one who sent Jesus when we refuse to destroy nature through unbridled consumerism. The Markan Jesus teaches us that we find Jesus and the one who sent Jesus incarnated in the kingdom of God that is the kingdom of nobodies.

So, inspired by these verses in Mark's gospel and Marguerite Porete's *Mirror of Simple Souls*, each chapter of this book is the theological refection of a historian of religions who specializes in Japanese Buddhism, Buddhist–Christian dialogue, and the current dialogue between science and religion in general, and Christian theology in particular. Accordingly, the thesis of chapter 2, "History of Religions: Methodology as Metaphor," is that the separation between historical studies of religious experience and theological reflection about the meaning of religious experience is a Cartesian dualism that needs to be rejected. That is, the usual separation between descriptive questions (e.g., what religious persons do and why they do it) and normative theological questions (e.g., the meaning and truth of what religious persons do) actually distorts the experiences of religious human beings.

My intention in chapter 3, "The Difficult Path," is to add my voice to a long list of writers seeking to relate Christian tradition to the hard realities of this post-Christian age of religious and secular pluralism by bringing Christian mystical theology into a discussion of the meaning of grace that, as a Lutheran, I think flows over this universe like a waterfall. Whitehead's philosophical vision provides a language that serves as a hermeneutical bridge by which historians of religions can interpret the teachings and practices of religious ways other than their own without falsification, and by which theologians can appropriate history-of-religions research as a means of helping Christians advance in their own faith journeys. The purpose of the journey of faith is what Whitehead called "creative transformation." The contemporary theological tradition that has most systematically and coherently followed Whitehead's lead in its refection on non-Christian Ways is process theology, which is the perhaps the only liberal or progressive theological movement now active in the twenty-first century.[2]

The thesis of chapter 4, "What's in a Name?" is that what Christians name God is elusively beyond the categories of theological reflection. But just because nothing we say or write literally applies to God does not imply that nothing meaningful can be said or written. After all, even mystics talked and wrote about God the way poets talk and write about love—in languages of unsaying that is nevertheless language. So the more I reflect on the process of "creative transformation" that I think is at work in humanity's collective religious Ways, as well as in the universe in general since the Big Bang 13.7 billion years ago, the more I am convinced that Alfred North Whitehead's model of God is on track because it provides a coherent vision for understanding the process of creative transformation at work in the pluralism of humanity's religious Ways.

---

2. See Dorrien, *The Making of American Liberal Theology*, chap. 4.

INTRODUCTION

Accordingly, chapter 4 is about the theological implications of religious and secular pluralism, where everywhere on this planet believers and unbelievers are in the same predicament, thrown back onto themselves in complex circumstances, looking for a sign. As ever, religious beliefs make claims somewhere between revelation and projection, somewhere between holiness and human frailty. But the problem of faith and belief for so long upheld by the plurality of human societies is now back on the individual, where it belongs. And if this is the case, individuals need to pay focused attention to the mystics who inhabit all religious Ways, who in their particular and often peculiar ways model a life of grace whose structure of existence the thirteenth-century French mystic Marguerite Porete characterized as "living without a why."

Chapter 5. "Butterfly in a Mirror," marks similarities and differences between Marguerite Porete's mystical theology, as recorded in *The Mirror of Simple Souls*, and the mystical philosophy of the Daoist sage Zuangzi, as recorded in the seven inner chapters of the *Zuangzi*—a work probably composed sometime between 530 and 275 BCE. While mystics in every religious Way are driven to countercultural and oftentimes severely nonconventional relationships to conventional and institutionalized religious traditions, all mystics remain grounded in the traditions that train them. Which means before mystical experiences occur, mystics are trained by the languages of their particular religious traditions about what they should look for before and after their experiences. There is no such thing as non-interpreted mystical experience. Christian, Buddhist, Hindu, and Muslim mystics described and wrote about the meaning of their experiences as Christians, Buddhists, Hindus, and Muslims. In other words, they all unconventionally engaged in the difficult path of theological reflection, or in the case of Buddhism, philosophical reflection. Christian theologians need to listen to and appropriate through dialogue these collective languages of unsaying.

Chapter 6, "A Theological Reflection on Mystical Experience," is a discussion of the general nature of mysticism and mystical experience. In the postmodern world we inhabit there can exist no one true faith evident at all times and in all places. Every religious tradition is merely one among many. The clear lines of orthodoxy in every religious Way are blurred by the pluralism of human experiences, are complicated by human lives.

Chapter 7, "The Jesus Way of Living without a Why," is a meditation on Marcus Borg's thesis that the historical Jesus was a Jewish mystic who taught a subversive wisdom that can be characterized as "living without a why."³ I also think that Pieter F. Craffert's depiction of the historical Jesus as a Jewish mystical shaman is quite credible, since many mystics cross-culturally—perhaps most—undergo shamanic experiences like visions, auditions, travels to other dimensions, out-of-body experiences, and healings of disease and of demon possession, which shamans experience cross-culturally.⁴ Like shamanic experiences, mystical experiences cross-culturally often involve vivid and sometimes frequent nonordinary states of conscious awareness and take a number of different forms. Sometimes, there is a vivid sense of journeying into another dimension of reality, which is the classic experience of shamans the world over.⁵ Sometimes, there is a strong sensation of another reality coming upon one, as in, "The Spirit fell upon me." Sometimes, an experience is of nature or of a natural object momentarily transfigured by the Sacred shining through it: Moses saw a burning bush that was not consumed; John of the Cross apprehended that the whole earth was filled with the "glory of God," where glory meant something like "radiant presence." In other words, in mystical experiences, the world is apprehended in such way that previous conventional perceptions seem like illusions.

In the concluding chapter, "Living without a Why: The Way of Grace," I argue that Christian mystical theology and Martin Luther's theological reflections are not experientially or conceptually far apart at all. Nor are Marguerite Porete's theology of "living without a why," Luther's theology of grace, and contemporary process theology experientially and conceptually far apart. We, and everything else caught in this space–time universe, do not exist outside our relationships. We become who we are only in complex relation to a network of other creatures at all times and in all places. In such a universe, doing theology is not identical with faith. It is faith's quest for understanding, an understanding that is never final, complete, or reducible to doctrines "once and for all delivered to the saints." Propositional certainty renders religious faith redundant. This is the most important lesson that the mystics who populate the Christian Way, from the historical Jesus to mystics like Marguerite Porete, teach us: if *faith* means "believing in doctrines," then faith shuts down the gospel. This is the error of Christian fundamentalism whenever and wherever it occurs. Thus, the only test for

---

3. Borg, *Meeting Jesus Again for the First Time*, 30.
4. Craffert, *The Life of a Galilean Shaman*, 43, 214–59.
5. See Eliade, *Shamanism*.

truthful faith is pragmatic: if truth is what sets us free, we can only recognize truth by its liberating effects.

TWO

History of Religions: Methodology as Metaphor

HISTORY OF RELIGIONS (*RELIGIONSWISSENSCHAFT*) traditionally defines its task as describing the totality of humanity's religious experience in all its historical manifestations. The founders of history of religions—Max Müller, Joachim Wach, Rudolf Otto, Max Weber, and later scholars like Mircea Eliade, Joseph Kitagawa, Huston Smith, and Wilfred Cantwell Smith—defined the goal of history of religions as understanding and describing how strong, how weak, and how enduring religious experience in ever new ways has manifested itself within the plurality of human cultural and historical experience. More specifically, history of religions is a collection of methods—ranging from historical studies to the multitude of social-scientific disciplines to evolutionary and neuroscientific theory—the collective goal of which is to describe how religious phenomena have evolved in human experience, both creatively and destructively, through what Joachim Wach called the "objective theoretical, practical, and sociological expressions of subjective religious experience."[1]

Note the implicit assumption: the phenomenal expressions of religious experience—its languages, cultic actions, and cultural and sociological expressions, along with the biological processes operating in the human brain—are codes that point to a transcendent religious reality: the Sacred, named differently in each religious tradition. Another way of stating this connection between phenomena and the Sacred, the way I personally prefer, is that the outward or phenomenal expressions of religious experience are metaphorical ways of figuring out the meaning of human experience of

1. Wach, *Sociology of Religion*, 19–34.

the Sacred. But, paradoxically, historians of religions are not typically interested in whether or not the phenomenal expressions of religious experience correspond to anything real beyond these expressions. Typically, such normative questions are not the object of a historian of religion's concern and are typically left to theologians and philosophers.

What begs for notice is the Cartesian epistemology that underlies history of religions as normally practiced. Description of what religious persons and communities do is divorced from questions about the meaning and truth of what religious persons and communities do. Accordingly, understanding (assumed by this methodological scheme) entails empirically describing religious phenomena. Such empirical description is separate from the normative issues of truth that actually operate in the lives of religious persons. In similarity with sociology, economics, and political science, history of religions is firmly grounded in Cartesian mind–body dualism.

This dualism became clear to me in my first teaching assignment at the University of California at Santa Barbra. Joseph M. Kitagawa, one of the foundational figures of history of religions, was a visiting professor in the spring semester of 1966, and I was lucky enough to be asked to be his teaching associate. One morning, I overheard a conversation between Professor Kitagawa and one of our students in our Introduction to Buddhism course. The student asked whether or not Buddhist doctrines of impermanence and suffering were "really true," and if so, whether these Buddhist teachings contradicted "the teachings of Christianity." Kitagawa's answer was that the student should consult with the theologians of the Religious Studies Department about normative truth questions, because history of religions is only concerned with empirically describing what religious people say they experience. "Whether or not the beliefs and practices of religious human beings correspond to reality are not the concern of historians of religions," he told this student. "For a historian of religions," he said, "*truth* means 'accurate description of what religious people have done and are now doing.' It has nothing to do with the truth of what religious human beings believe have done or do."

This compartmentalization of knowledge has troubled me ever since. As anyone who has taught undergraduate students soon realizes, comparing religious practices, ethical teachings, myths, rituals, doctrines, history, or social-political-communal expressions of religious human beings and communities does not erase difficult methodological problems internal to the practice of history of religions that in fact involve normative questions. First are quantitative difficulties. The sheer amount of material available for historical investigation is simply too vast for any single historian of religions to manage or master. Consequently, historians of religions are forced to depend on the research of numerous experts in more specialized fields of religious study such as ethnology, psychology of religion, sociology of religions, and anthropology, and on the insights of specialists in specific religious traditions such as Islamic studies, Indian studies, Buddhist studies, Confucian-Daoist studies, Japanese religions, Judaism, aboriginal studies—and yes, even neuroscience. In an age of academic specialization, history of religions has since its early infancy defined itself as an interdisciplinary field. Currently, historians of religions emphasize the methods of the social sciences, particularly sociology of religion.

Besides quantitative problems, historians of religions also encounter qualitative issues having to do with the uniqueness of foreign inwardness, which is always ingredient in religious traditions other than one's own. As Wilfred Cantwell Smith noted, if it is not possible to understand, even partially, religious experience other than one's own, then history of religions has no justification for its existence.[2] But how is it possible, without falsification, to get into these traditions so that they can be described to those who do not participate in them? How can we bridge the cultural and historical gaps between our history and culture and the history and culture embodied in the religious traditions we are seeking to empirically describe? Such questions are not unique to history of religions. All scholarly disciplines are burdened with the same problems—interrelating abstract empirical description with what human beings report they actually experience.

In spite of these difficulties, historians of religions are agreed that at least partial understanding is possible. Understanding is always a matter of degree because the phenomenal expressions of religious experience cross-culturally—myths, rituals, teachings, and practices—seem to allow something of their inner meaning to shine through for those who know how to look. The depth of understanding achieved depends on the research skills, luck, and intuitive sensitivity of individual historians of religions.

Furthermore, the point of departure for history of religions is that whatever else it may be, religion cannot be understood in terms of nonreligious factors. That is, all forms of reductionism that seek to explain religion in terms not particular to religion itself explain nothing by explaining

---

2. W. C. Smith, *The Meaning and End of Religion*, chap. 2.

religion away. The problem is that, as Wilfred Cantwell Smith, Robert Bellah, and others have noted, there exists no such thing as *religion* (as a noun abstracted from the actual concrete lives of religious human beings).[3] Do definitions of religion cover all the ways human beings have been or are now religious? Most probably not. Which means that defining *religion* is a bit like defining *pornography*. In the same way we recognize pornography, so we know religion when we see it.

The simplest way to verify that the moment one attempts to define *religion* one creates a reductionist abstraction having little to do with the experiences of religious human beings is to ask a group of people (say, undergraduate or graduate students in a course on Buddhism) to define *religion*. Most begin by saying, "Religion is the worship of God," which leaves out Buddhism, significant parts of Hinduism, and Confucian and Daoist traditions, because the word *God* has quite different meanings in each of these traditions—and in Buddhism's nontheistic worldview, no positive meaning at all. After a while, the discussion simply runs out of gas. As one of my students once asked:

"So Professor Ingram, you teach courses in religion, but you don't know what religion is?"

"Yes," I answered.

Can a football or basketball game engender religious experiences for some fans? A rock concert or an opera? Suddenly arriving at a conclusion to a difficult mathematical equation after a long struggle? What Einstein experienced when he finally arrived at his special and general theories of relativity? Reading with understanding the poetry of William Butler Yeats or John Keats or Emily Dickinson? Why are these experiences any less religious than what faithful Christians might experience attending a liturgy in a Lutheran, Catholic, or Episcopal church, or than what the Buddha experienced sitting under the Tree of Awakening?

In other words, there is a staggering amount of data, phenomena, and human experiences and expressions that might be characterized in one culture or another, by one criterion or another, as religious; but there is no universally valid definition of *religion*. *Religion* as a noun seems to be an abstraction divorced from the actual experiences of religious human beings, an abstraction created by scholars during the Western Enlightenment solely for use in the scholar's study, for the scholar's analytic purposes. It would seem that the term *religion* has no existence apart from its use in the

---

3. See ibid., chap. 4; and Bellah, *Religion in Human Evolution*, preface.

academy. Still, while it is true that many societies (including, for example, Islamic societies) do not draw clear lines between their culture and what scholars would call religion, this does not mean that religious experiences are illusions.

In this regard, it's worth keeping in mind that when we think we have a handle on what religion is, we may be fooling ourselves. Definitions of *religion* tend to suffer from one of two problems: either they are too narrow (and exclude experiences many or most persons experience as religious), or they are too vague and ambiguous (and so suggest that just about any and everything is religious).

But there is another methodological hiccup. Historians of religions cannot do their work without some prior notion of what it is they are seeking to understand. The problem is not so much getting rid of a methodological framework, but reflectively and creatively employing a methodological point of departure so that something concrete can be revealed and said about religious experience that relates to the lives of real persons. Any methodological approach will undergo adjustments over time as historians of religions do their work. This means that historians of religions should self-consciously specify the wider philosophical worldview assumed by their methodologies. The worldview assumed by most historians of religions now working in the field is Cartesian dualism and its resulting epistemology.

So historians of religions confront two questions: What makes something religious? and How is this religious something best understood? These two questions are utterly interdependent, because how we define what makes something religious is a reflection of the worldview assumed by the methods we employ to understand the something we think is religious. Conversely, the methods we employ to understand the something we think is religious reflect our prior assumptions about what makes something religious. In what follows, accordingly, I shall try to make explicit my tacit understanding of what it is that I am talking, writing, or teaching about when I think I'm confronted by something religious. Following this, I shall focus on clarifying the philosophical assumptions underlying my methodological approach to the practice of history of religions—assumptions that rest on the process philosophy of Alfred North Whitehead.

What Makes Something Religious?

As readers can by now guess, I often wonder if very much depends on a definition of *religion* since *religion* is an abstraction that exists in the heads of scholars and has little, if anything, to do with the experiences of actual religious human beings. Can definitions tell people whether or not they are religious? If so, why is it that religious persons do not seem concerned about a definition that summarizes what they are doing? I have through the years come to the realization that the issues here are more fundamental than a problem in semantics. Many notions of religion are possible so long as they are coherently and nondogmatically employed. With this in mind, I shall describe four elements that, when I perceive them conjoined together, cause me to think, there's something religious going on here.

First, religious traditions express a vision of the world, of "the way things really are," which is not given in ordinary sensory (meaning, "empirical") experience. Religious visions of reality have usually included entities superior to or beyond the natural world: that is, gods, God, spirits, demonic beings, angels, and other sorts of entities. A religious vision may also be experienced as a change of perspective about the nature of the world and of one's deepest self from an unenlightened to an enlightened state of consciousness, as (for example) in Theravada Buddhism; in Mahayana Buddhism; in some forms of Hinduism such as Advaita Vedanta; in Confucian and Daoist practice; and in Jewish, Christian, and Islamic mysticism. Whenever human nature is understood to imply soul, spirit, Buddha Nature, Brahman-Atman, or something other than what is accessible to ordinary sensory experience, we have encountered something religious.

Second, for religious human beings something exists (or perhaps many things exist) whose value and validity are neither measurable nor attainable by means of the pragmatic concerns of daily living. Religious human beings apprehend a dimension of truth and value that does not require anything other than itself in order to present concurrent social and moral obligations. Some goal of supreme value is to be attained, individually and communally, that transcends the relativity of all other purposes. This sense of ultimacy is what I understand Mircea Eliade meant by the Sacred, and what Rudolf Otto meant by the Holy.

Third, all means of expressing religious apprehension of "the way things really are" and how human beings should properly live in accordance with "the way things really are" are necessarily symbolic, even though some religious persons (for example, fundamentalists) interpret their symbols and myths literally. All cumulative traditions express their particular sense of the Sacred through standardized forms of private and public ritual. Perceptions of a supreme reality, or power, or excellence beyond the givens of everyday concerns and obligations is acknowledged, talked about, and ritually celebrated.

Presupposed here, of course, is the existence of common human characteristics cross-culturally and biologically that serve as the foundation of one religious person's understanding of another. Something in common is present, even though historians of religions are not in agreement about what this something is, or about how it an be empirically described. As Kitagawa once noted, most historians of religions are either "historically oriented" or "phenomenologically oriented."[4] Historically oriented scholars tend to be concerned about what really happened and about the actual becoming of particular religious phenomena so that the data of religious experience can be empirically described in historical interconnection with other cumulative traditions, past and present. Phenomenologically oriented scholars (for example, Mircea Eliade) are most likely to search for the structures common to all forms of religious experience past and present. In this approach, the data of religious experience are dealt with cross-culturally and typologically without much regard to historical and cultural nuances.

Finally, religious persons do not accept the world as given in ordinary states of awareness. To the question, is this all there is? religious human beings cross-culturally—since Paleolithic cave-dwellers painted the shapes of animals on the walls of caves in France forty thousand years ago—have answered, no. Cumulative traditions, wherever they are found, are about seeking and attaining transformative experiences of a different sort from normal individual and/or communal experiences in everyday existence. The means of achieving such experiences—ritually reenacting myths, reading biographies of holy men and women, reading or hearing scriptures, praying, meditating, taking part in liturgies or in community activism, celebrating sacred times or holidays, observing funeral rites—are all means of raising consciousness of a Sacred reality, in, with, and under the givens of ordinary experience, which in themselves are as boring as they are predictable.

Accordingly, at the very minimum, religious faith or religious experience names what binds individuals and communities together to what is experienced as a sacred reality both immanent within and transcendent

---

4. Kitagawa, "Primitive, Classical, and Modern Religions," 39–41.

to the universe. Whether encountered through participation in public worship services; through contemplative prayer, meditation, or activist engagement; or through the mystical experiences described in all cumulative traditions, religious experience is what binds human beings and human communities together to a reality that is more than that posited by ordinary experience. This reality is literally beyond names yet has many names: God, Allah, Brahman, YHWH, Krishna, Vishnu, Buddha Nature, Wakan-Tanka, Spirit—and, yes, Nature.

It is here that one encounters the problem with descriptive phenomenological studies. The avowed goal of history of religions is one of descriptively understanding religious phenomena as they really are, apart from concern with normative theological and philosophical issues. But this goal divorces descriptive accounts of religious experiences from what religious persons and communities believe they actually experience. Religious human beings *do not* experience what scholars describe and conclude that they experience. Or restated in terms of the topic of this book, what mystics claim about their experience is not identical with scholarly accounts of what Christian or Muslim mystics experience as union or oneness with God. Nor is what monks or nuns experience in a Zen temple identical with scholarly accounts of what Zen Buddhists experience as "Emptying" (*śūnyatā*). The goal for historians of religions is objective description of religious phenomena, setting forth the facts, of religious experience in isolation from the subjective experiences of religious human beings. Again, the operational model here is Cartesian: the goal is knowledge established by disinterested cognition of empirically perceived religious facts that exist independently of the knower and indeed are in no way affected by being known or unknown.

What I am objecting to here is the notion of objectivity presupposed by not only historians of religions, but also most scholars in all academic fields of inquiry, which has been the norm in Western academic scholarship since the sixteenth century. What I am arguing for is that realist notions of objectivity need to be reformulated by means of a nominalist or constructivist understanding of objectivity that does not separate the knower from what is known.

By *constructivism* I mean, first, a particular way of understanding the relation between what we call knowledge and what we experience as reality, "the way things really are."[5] Constructivist accounts of cognition conceive the specific features of what we experience and think about as the world (objects, entities, boundaries, properties, categories) not as prior to or independent of our sensory, perceptual, and conceptual activities but as emerging from—that is, as *constructed by*—these activities."[6]

Second, constructivist accounts of cognitive processes—including cognitive dissonance and boundary questions—understand beliefs, not as particular correct or incorrect propositions about mental representations of the world, but as linked perceptual dispositions and behavioral routines continuously strengthened, weakened, and reconfigured through continual interaction with the cultural, social, economic, educational, historical, and religious environments in which we live. This epistemological point of view is the opposite of Cartesian-like referential epistemologies that conceive knowledge as a match between statements of belief about matters of fact residing in an external world. According to constructivist epistemologies, truth is a "situation of relatively stable and effective mutual coordination among socially constructed statements, beliefs, experiences, and practical values."[7]

In other words, knowledge is a system of beliefs that have become relatively well established within particular social and cultural environments. Knowledge and beliefs, like new species of life evolving from previous species in evolutionary theory, emerge from at least three interdependent sets of forces: (1) individual and communal perceptual and behavioral activities and experiences, (2) general cognitive processes originating in the human brain's biological structure cross-culturally, and (3) particular social or collective systems of thought and procedures. In this way, knowledge and its accompanying systems of beliefs are contingently shaped and multiply constrained.[8]

Constructivist epistemologies do not deny an external reality beyond the subjective mental process occurring in the human brain. Instead, constructivist epistemologies assume that specific features of human interaction with reality are not prior to or independent of subjective mental processes but emerge from and acquire their specific meanings through them. Given

---

5. I have summarized a constructivist epistemology in Ingram, *Theological Reflection at the Boundaries*, 20–22.

6. See B. H. Smith, *Scandalous Knowledge*, 3.

7. Ibid., 4.

8. Ibid., 11.

this intimate connection between subjective mental processes and perception of reality, no particular method exists that universally characterizes, for example, scientific method or theological method, or philosophical method, or method in history of religions, because the activities of scientists, theologians, philosophers, and historians of religions are pluralistic. So these pluralistic methods include much that realists or foundationalists view as unscientific and nontheological (i.e. having to do with biological, social, economic, scientific, and historical efforts and contexts).

When applied to the practice of history of religions (or theology, for that matter), the idea that a historian of religions should seek disinterested, impersonal, descriptive knowledge about religious matters of fact independently of human experience of these matters of fact makes little sense. As I have argued, the realist epistemologies assumed by most working historians of religions tend to create abstractions divorced from the lives of religious human beings. Accordingly, in what follows I shall argue that process philosophy, particularly as embodied in the traditions of Alfred North Whitehead and Charles Hartshorne, provide for historians of religions willing to listen a hermeneutical bridge by which to interpret humanity's religious experience that does not create the usual Cartesian dualisms between religious phenomena and what real human beings actually experience. An added benefit for Christian theological reflection is that history of religions refigured in terms of process philosophy provides a general worldview that allows Christian theologians to dialogically engage the practices, teachings, and experiences of non-Christians in a way that does not falsify what non-Christians actually practice, affirm, and experience. This non-Christian data then becomes the foundation for Christian dialogue with the world's religions minus the traditional theological imperialism that has been ingredient in Christian interactions with non-Christians for two thousand years.

A Process Approach to History of Religions

We live in a religiously plural world. Our neighbors represent an incredible diversity of religious traditions, perspectives, and practices. In my neck of the universe, a Thai Buddhist temple with a resident community of monks was dedicated in Federal Way, Washington, in 2000. This beautiful temple, surrounded by huge groves of Douglas firs and western hemlocks, attracts thousands of Theravada Buddhists to its festivals. In Tacoma, the Korean community built a large Buddhist temple. The resident community of monks practices Korean Zen, and instruction is offered to anyone interested in learning Korean Zen meditation. In the main temple stands a large image of the Buddha of Infinite Light. Three blocks from my Lutheran community at Our Redeemer's Lutheran Church in Seattle stands a large Baptist church that was sold to the Tibetan community who transformed the building into the Tibetan Buddhist Temple. On the Interstate 5 corridor, from Bellingham to Vancouver, Washington, the number of immigrant Buddhist temples, Hindu temples, Jewish synagogues, and Sikh temples is almost beyond counting. Our Redeemer's Lutheran Church is in a creative dialogue with the Amidi Muslim Community in Lakewood, Washington. So our neighbors are Buddhists, Hindus, Muslims, Jews, Sikhs, Christians from all denominations, Native Americans, Wiccans, and fundamentalist secularists, who think religion is illusory, a waste of time.

Here lies the problem: relating descriptive *how* questions generated by religious diversity to normative *why* questions that religious diversity engenders. As I have argued, *why* questions are not normally the business of historians of religions. We are trained to deal with descriptive *how* questions, in much the same way that natural scientists are concerned with describing the *how* questions that explain the origins and physical realities that account for the physical structures of the universe. *Why* the universe is as it is cannot be answered by means of scientific methods of investigation. The moment a scientist engages with a *why* question, that scientist becomes a theologian or philosopher. This does not mean that *why* questions are unimportant or that scientists should not engage them.

Similarly, the methodologies of historians of religion can actually engage descriptive *how* and *why* questions. But this requires wearing two methodological hats simultaneously. For example, how do religious traditions and practices reflect the history and social structures of a particular community? How do the history and social structures of a community affect a religious tradition's historical development? What does evolutionary biology, particularly the neurosciences, tell us about the origins of religion and the physical foundations of religious experience? What are the similarities and the differences between the world's religious traditions? And the list goes on. But the methods of history of religions are as unsuitable for dealing with normative or *why* and *ought* questions as rational reflection is for resolving a Zen Buddhist koan.

Examples abound. To which religious tradition ought persons commit? Do Buddhist teachings and practices accurately reflect the structures of existence? Do Christian or Jewish or Muslim or Hindu or Chinese traditions? Can any religious tradition be judged as truer than the rest? These sorts of normative questions require theological reflection *at the boundaries*—or if one is a nontheist, philosophical reflection *at the boundaries*—that join conventional ways of knowing with the language or "unsaying" employed by mystics in all the world's religious traditions.[9] Any solution also requires engagement in interreligious dialogue that also, in my opinion, requires dialogue with the natural sciences as a third partner.[10]

This is why I am *not* asserting that historians of religions should disengage from theological or philosophical *why* questions. Scholars in my field should refuse to be limited by the Cartesian dualisms that balkanize academic disciplines into territories having no relationship other than being other. So in protest against this ghettoizing of knowledge fields, I have consciously chosen to wear two methodological hats: that of a historian of religions and that of a Lutheran theologian informed by his work in history of religions and by his dialogue with the natural sciences. *How* questions and *why* questions, descriptive questions and normative questions, are utterly interdependent.

The religious diversity that surrounds me in the Pacific Northwest is typical of the religious diversity surrounding the vast majority of human beings alive today. The term *religious diversity* names the fact of the existence of differing religious traditions, practices, and experiences that surround persons no matter what their own religious commitments, practices, or cultural heritage might be. But the term *pluralism* is not merely another name for diversity.[11] Pluralism goes beyond mere diversity. Religious diversity is an observable fact all over the world. But without engagement with one another, the mere fact of the existence of neighboring churches, temples and mosques are just trivial examples of diversity. This is so because pluralism is not an empirical fact. Pluralism is an attitude, a theological-philosophical orientation, a theoretical construct that seeks to coherently interpret the meaning of the data of religious diversity that is the object of research for historians of religions.

As a theoretical construct, pluralism is neither an ideology nor a Western neoliberal scheme nor a debilitating form of relativism. Pluralism

---

9. See Ingram, *Theological Reflections at the Boundaries*, chap. 1.

10. See Ingram, *Buddhist-Christian Dialogue in an Age of Science*, chaps. 1–2.

11. For a more detailed description of the structure of the experience of religious pluralism, see Ingram, *Theological Reflections at the Boundaries*, 28–29.

is best understood as a dynamic process through which we dialogically engage with one another through our very deepest difference. Nor is pluralism mere tolerance of the other, but rather an active attempt to understand the other. Although tolerance is a step forward from intolerance, it does not require neighbors to know one another. Tolerance can create a climate of restraint, but not understanding. This is so because tolerance does little to overcome the stereotypes and fears that govern the lives of many religious persons when they encounter the religious other. Pluralism is a theological-philosophical move beyond tolerance based on exclusivist and inclusivist theologies of religions toward constructive understanding of what to make of the empirical facts of religious diversity gathered by historians of religions.[12]

Just as pluralism is not synonymous with tolerance, so pluralism does not imply debilitating relativism. It does not displace deep religious or secular commitments because pluralism is the serious encounter with religious commitments. Many critics of pluralism persist in linking pluralism with a kind of valueless relativism in which all perspectives are equally compelling, and, as a result equally uncompelling. Pluralism, they contend, undermines commitment to one's own particular faith tradition with its own particular language by watering down particularity in the interest of universality. I consider this interpretation a distortion of the meaning of pluralism. Pluralism is engagement with, not abdication of, differences and particularities. Thus, while encountering persons of other faiths may lead to a less myopic view of one's own faith, pluralism is not premised on reductive relativism.

Finally, the language of pluralism is dialogue. Dialogue is vital to the health of a religious community so that we can appropriate our faith, not by relying on habit or heritage alone, but by making our faith our own within the context of encounter with persons of other faith traditions. The goal of interreligious dialogue is not agreement but relationship. As the language of pluralism, dialogue is the language of engagement, involvement, and participation.

The difference between religious diversity and religious pluralism that I have outlined reflects my agreement with Alfred North Whitehead's conception of God. Three elements of Whitehead's metaphysics are germane to

---

12. See Ingram, *Wrestling with the Ox*, chap. 2; and Ingram, *The Modern Buddhist–Christian Dialogue*, chap. 2, for my critique of exclusivist and inclusivist theologies of religions.

his understanding of God. First is the category of creativity, which Whitehead described as the "universal of universals," meaning that process by which every particular entity in the universe (the "disjunctive diversity" of the universe) enters into complex unity with everything in the universe (the "conjunctive oneness" of the universe). That is, the many actual occasions (all things and events at every moment of space–time) constituting the disjunctive diversity of the universe become one actual occasion: the universe conjunctively.[13]

What this implied for Whitehead is that creativity is also the principle of novelty. All things and events are particular, novel entities distinct from every other entity in the universe that the universe experientially unifies. Yet since every actual occasion (every thing and event, or every society of things and events) unifies the many constituents of the universe itself in its own distinctive way according to its particular "subjective aim" to achieve the fullest "satisfaction" of which it is capable, creativity is a process that always introduces novelty into the content of the of the many things and events that constitute the universe conjunctively.[14]

By implication, the creative processes at play in the universe have no independent existence apart from the actual things and events in the universe undergoing process. Therefore, as "categorically ultimate," all things and events undergo the universal process of creativity, including that actual occasion Whitehead named God, and that historians of religions like Eliade and Kitagawa rather generically named the Sacred. That is, all things and events, including God (the Sacred), are concrete instances of the "many becoming one and increased by one."[15]

While all things and events exemplify the process of creativity particularized according to their own "subjective aim," even if only trivially, Whitehead thought that God is the formative element, indeed the chief example, of the creative process. Accordingly, he wrote of God's reality as "bi-polar," as constituted by two interdependent "natures": an eternal, unchanging "primordial nature," and a changing, processive "consequent nature." God's primordial nature is God's everlasting self-identity through time, what constitutes God as God throughout the moments of God's experiences as God. God's consequent nature is what God becomes as

---

13. Whitehead, *Process and Reality*, 16, 141; Whitehead, *Science and the Modern World*, 153–53; and Whitehead, *Modes of Thought*, 31.

14. Whitehead, *Process and Reality*, 31–32.

15. Ibid.

God affects and is affected by the multiplicity of past and present things and events according to God's "subjective aim" that all things and events achieve maximum intensity and harmony of experience.[16] In other words God's consequent nature is what God becomes as God experiences and interrelates with every thing and event in the universe, while God's primordial nature is an abstraction from the actual process of what God is in God's consequent nature. Both natures are interdependent and mutually constitute what God is in God's own experience of the universe—and the universe's experience of God.

Finally, God, according to Whitehead, is the source of novelty and order in the universe. The source of novelty is God's primordial envisaging of pure possibilities coupled with God's desire that these possibilities be realized in their due season, which is part of the initial aim God gives to all actual occasions of experience—which may or may not be taken into account by an occasion's subjective aim for itself. Novelty is an actualization of new possibilities that generally increases the enjoyment of experience because the variety of possibilities that are actualized in the universe add richness, texture, zest, and intensity to both God's and an occasion's experiences. The source of God's continuing creation of novelty originates in this process of God's interaction with every actual occasion in the universe, past and present, as God lures all occasions to achieve the fullest satisfaction of which they are capable.

But novel possibilities cannot be realized in the universe in simply any order because some novel possibilities can become real only sequentially after other novel possibilities have been realized. That is, at one stage of becoming, novel possibilities are realized for the first time, and if they are repeated, they become part of the order of the universe that contextualizes the actualization of future possibilities. Thus God is the source of order because order represents the dominance of a novel element in the universe, so that God is the source of novelty. God is also the source of order in the universe because neither order nor novelty is intrinsically good, but instrumental to the one intrinsic good, which is "enjoyment of intense experience." In Whitehead's words, "God's purpose in the creative advance is the evocation of societies of actual occasions and is purely subsidiary to this end."[17]

16. Ibid., 531–33.

17. Ibid., 533ff. It should be noted that this aspect of Whitehead's metaphysics was deeply influenced by quantum physics and evolutionary biology.

Translating these aspects of Whitehead's conception of God into the methodological framework of history of religions, I propose that the Sacred is the source of order and novelty in the universe to which the particular religious traditions of humanity refer in their distinctive experiences, teachings, and practices, named differently by each tradition. Some cumulative traditions have emphasized (i.e., "prehended") the nonpersonal dimensions of the Sacred as ineffable (beyond the ability of language—definitions, doctrines, symbols—to fully grasp and conceptually express). Examples of the Sacred as ineffable include Brahman in most Upanishadic Hinduism, or Emptying in Mahayana Buddhism, or the Dao or "Way" in Daoist tradition. Other examples include Islamic Sufi mysticism, Jewish Kabbalah, and Christian mystical tradition. Persons who participate in these traditions seek to experience a connection between themselves and the Sacred conceived as nonpersonally transcendent to, yet immanent within, all finite things and events, by means of such disciplines as yoga, meditation, and (in monotheistic traditions) centering and contemplative prayer.

The vast majority of human beings have experienced (i.e., "prehended") the Sacred through a range of specific deities. Judging from the Paleolithic cave paintings in the Grotto of Lascaux in France, experience of the Sacred as a personal deity or a personal set of deities with whom one is in relationship probably represents the most archaic expression of religious experience. Yet no one has ever encountered the Sacred as nonpersonal *in general*, or as personal *in general*. We never experience anything in general but only in particular, always bounded by historically and culturally situated images and symbols. For as there are different ways of being human, so it is within the contexts of history and culture that the presence of the Sacred as personal or nonpersonal is experienced pluralistically.

Christians experience the Sacred as personal through narratives of the life, death, and resurrection of the historical Jesus of Nazareth confessed to be the Christ. Christians trust these narratives about the relation between human beings and God the Father and the Father's continuing work in the world through the Holy Spirit. Similarly, Jews bet their lives on the gift of Yahweh's Torah ("instructions") and the resulting covenant between Jews and God through Moses on Mount Sinai. Muslims surrender their wills (*'islām*) to Allah as recited by the Prophet Muhammed in the Qur'an, "the Book wherein there is no doubt," wherein Muslims believe is recorded the "straight way" of humanity's most complete religion. In Hindu devotional faith, the Sacred is experienced as Siva, Vishnu, Kali, Rama—through as many forms of Brahman ("Sacred Power") as you please. Mahayana Buddhists, perhaps the majority, encounter the Dharma beyond name and form masked by a multiplicity of Bodhisattvas. Aboriginal people encounter the Sacred personified in wind, rain, mountains, lakes, rivers, sun, moon, stars, and the natural rhythms of growth and decay.

Yet, there is always something nonpersonal about personalized experience of the Sacred. It is not just that the deities often interrelate with nature and human beings nonpersonally: Jesus is reported to have said that like rain, God's love for creation is disinterested and falls on the just and the unjust, so don't take it personally. Images of the Sacred (for example, the icons of Orthodox Christianity) also reveal that the Sacred is infinitely beyond the scope of human understanding and historical and cultural perspective. And yet as both the nontheistic and theistic religious ways of humanity teach, just because we cannot know *everything* about the Sacred does not mean that we cannot know *something*, since according the Whiteheadian version of religious pluralism that I have described in this chapter, the Sacred, however it is named, is always interacting with the particulars of the universe as the source of ordered novelty. Some of this ordered novelty is encountered in humanity's religious traditions.

Of course *how* cumulative traditions name the Sacred they experience within bounded historical and cultural perspectives is a mater of crucial importance, not only for a cumulative tradition's collective self-understanding, but also for how cumulative traditions teach their adherents to interact with other cumulative traditions. In Christian tradition, this *how* is called theology. An illustration of how Christian theology can be creatively transformed by history of religions is the topic of the next chapter.

THREE

The Difficult Path

It is well to begin this chapter with a wonderful observation by Mary Midgley: "We know that it is vanishingly unlikely that a single way of thinking will ever explain the world's workings completely. No one pattern of thought—not even in physics—is so 'fundamental' that all others will eventually be reduced to it. For most questions a number of conceptual toolboxes always have to be used together. And there is no single law showing us how we should combine theme."[1] One of the reasons Midgley is, I think, on track is the reality of boundary questions that engender the experience of cognitive dissonance in all disciplines of thought. There are always knowledge boundaries in all disciplines, particularly in the natural sciences and theological reflection.

This is so because methods of inquiry (for example, scientific methods or methods of theological reflection) always raise questions incapable of solutions by the application of their peculiar methodologies. Cognitive dissonance occurs when competing conclusions established by identical or different methodological principles clash, as in, for example, the cognitive dissonance Albert Einstein experienced when Niels Bohr and Werner Heisenberg began looking at the uncertainties involved in quantum physics. In the realm of the very large, relativity is currently the best option. But in the realm of the very small, quantum physics wins the day. The cognitive dissonance of this clash of physical theories now engenders a search for a quantum theory of gravity that might harmonize relativity and quantum theories. To this date, the search is ongoing.

I often wonder when the biologists will reject reductionist, determinist interpretations of evolutionary theory—particularly those rooted

1. Midgley, "Concluding Reflections," 969.

in materialist interpretations of natural selection—and catch up with the physicists. I also wonder when theologians will become aware of the boundaries of knowledge in theological reflection, particularly when speaking and writing about God: the ultimate boundary condition. Christian fundamentalism and most evangelical theology ignore the boundary constraints of God-talk and thereby foster enormous cognitive dissonance among faithful Christians and non-Christians, as well as secularist skeptics as they cling to their particular worldviews. As our Buddhist brothers and sisters instruct, if we are able to hear, clinging to anything is the cause of great suffering for human beings and for the creatures with whom we must share this planet. Nonclinging is the Buddhist version of what Marguerite Porete called "living without a why," a way of life that is descriptive of Christian experience of grace.

Consequently, the practice of Christian theological reflection means entering a very difficult path because it requires letting go of one's theological constructions even as one has worked hard at creating theological constructions. While the following is not an exhaustive description, here are a few of the problems facing anyone engaged in theological reflection.

First, it is not possible to speak of God without having experienced an interior silence. The difficulty is that speaking or writing about God is unlike anything else we can speak or write about because God is not a thing or an object that can be captured by the words of any language system. Reflection about God, written or spoken, creates a discourse about our entire being in interdependence with all beings in the universe and with God.

Second, discourse about God is not the monopoly of any religious tradition. But within the context of Christian tradition, meaningful theological construction is always reflection by grace through faith alone. At least this seems true to me as a Lutheran and an avid reader of the Synoptic Gospels and the Epistles of Saint Paul. But thinking and speaking about God is a pluralistic process and is the reason why God cannot be the monopoly of any religious tradition or of any subtradition within a religious tradition.

Third, theological reflection is not reducible to doctrinal formulations. This is so because theological language is always symbolic, never literal. Since we cannot understand or signify what the word *God* means in terms of a single perspective, interreligious dialogue is the heart of authentic theological reflection in an age of religious pluralism.

Finally, theological discourse completes itself by entering what Thomas Merton called "the Silence." Entering the silence requires shutting up in order to be opened up by the mystery that is God, which all theological reflection invariably conceals. That is, Christian theologians invariably end up confronted by that wordless experience of God's grace, which Marguerite Porete described as "living without a why." This implies that theological reflection says more about us than about God, which does not mean that theological reflection does not symbolically point to what the reality of God is or is not. But we should not cling to our pointers—our doctrines, symbols, or distinctive religious practices as "the only way." If we do, we only have the doctrinal pointers.

What theologians reflect upon is a transcendent reality named God, if one is reflecting in English. But the problem is that a God that is completely transcendent can't be conceived or spoken about, and would be utterly superfluous to the universe in general and to human experience in particular. A completely transcendent God is a denial of divine immanence, which also simultaneously destroys human transcendence. And yet while God is ultimately ineffable mystery, this need not mean we can't say *something* about God even though we can't say everything there is to say. Just because we can't know or say everything doesn't mean we can't know or say something meaningful. For transcendence and immanence, for God and beings created in the image of God, are interdependent. Transcendence reflects God's "primordial nature," as Whitehead described it, while God's immanence names God's "consequent nature."

So those engaged in theological reflection intentionally makes life quite difficult for themselves and for others, for their work is much more difficult than the work of historians of religions. Nor do theologians follow the alleged easy route taken by the natural scientists: remain skeptical until empirical confirmation requires belief. I think Christian theologians particularly have been victimized by revelation. God has visited the earth; the transcendent has visited the immanent in the life, death, and resurrection of a Galilean peasant two thousand years ago. The mysterious and unfathomable is simultaneously natural and partially understandable, provided that we wrestle with God as seriously as Jacob is said to have wrestled with God at the River Jabbok (Gen 32:24–31). And just as the wrestling match is said to have left Jacob limping, so wrestling with God will leave us limping as well.

So if revelation has indeed visited the earth in the life, death, and resurrection of a Galilean peasant two thousand years ago, this visitation has done theologians few favors. What we might wish from revelation is a window though which to glimpse the visible landscape of the transcendent. But the window remains shut, and like a "mirror of simple souls" turns us back to gaze on our own mundane reality. All revelation does is remind us that there is a sacred reality transcendent to and immanent within our world. But to know exhaustively what this sacred reality actually is remains impossible within the scope of knowledge circumscribed by the universe we inhabit. Mystics in all the world's cumulative traditions agree on this point, and Christian theological reflection must start here.

So as a historian of religions engaged in theological reflection, I too have been victimized by revelation, particularly by the revelatory claims of Christian fundamentalists and their political cronies on the religious Right in North America. On the religious Right are many conservative Protestant churches, numerous theologians and pastors in my own Lutheran tradition (who ought to know better), and televangelists using pulpits for financial gain through the sale of theological snake oil. Such organizations wear me out because of the ways they not only reduce Christian faith to a set of doctrines (the commitment to which is necessary before one can wear the label *Christian*) but also reduce God to a Republican Party hack.

Furthermore, what we might call Christian beliefs differ so profoundly that I am often not sure what being a Christian means. This is why over the past few years I have refused to describe my faith with the label *Christian*. According to fundamentalist labels—and according to the prosperity gospel, because I am not wealthy—I am not a Christian. Nor do I wish to be if being a Christian requires commitment to such utter nonsense. Furthermore, according to Roman Catholic doctrine, at best I am an anonymous Christian when my beliefs and behavior are similar to the teachings of Roman Catholicism. So if being a Christian means committing to the belief systems of some particular ideological or institutional system defined as Christian, I am not a Christian. Although I am highly critical of the theology of Karl Barth, I agree with Barthian theologian Douglas John Hall: Christian faith is reducible to neither a system of doctrines nor a system of morality nor a particular ecclesiastical institution.[2]

For me, the problem is the reduction of faith to adherence to a doctrinal system. Christianity is the only cumulative tradition in the world's religions traditions that practices theological reflection centered on formulating and defending doctrinal propositions. Christianity inherited this practice from classical Greek philosophy as the early Jesus movement translated itself

---

2. Hall, *What Christianity Is Not*, chaps. 3–5.

into the intellectual context of Hellenistic culture, beginning with Saint Paul. But anyone thinking that religious faith requires craven clinging to a fixed, unalterable, self-evident set of doctrines or to the Bible should "read the rabbis."[3] Midrash required the rabbis to investigate and go in search of fresh insight. So the rabbis used, and still use, the Tanakh, not to retreat into the past, but to propel them into the uncertainties of the post-temple world. Jews built an intellectual bridge between the past and the continually changing present as they creatively reinterpreted the available authoritative biblical texts to carry Jewish tradition forward into the future, with the result that the rabbis stressed the centrality of compassion and justice in community as a way of following the Torah. Jewish faith is never defined by belief in Jewish doctrines.

Nor does the New Testament define faith as belief in doctrines. Christian theological teaching until the fourth century (when Christianity was declared a legal religion in the Roman empire by Constantine) did not understand faith as belief in doctrinal propositions. When the New Testament was translated from Greek into Latin by Jerome (c. 342–420) the Greek *pistis* ("trust") became the Latin *fides* ("loyalty"). The Latin *fides* has no verbal form, so for the Greek *pisteuō* Jerome used the Latin verb *credo*, which is derived from *cor do* ("I give my heart"). Jerome did not use *opinor* ("I hold an opinion"). When the Bible was translated into English, *credo* and *pisteuō* became "I believe" in the King James Version (1611). But the meaning of the word *belief* has changed over the centuries. In Middle English, *bileven* meant "to prize," "to value," "to hold dear." It was related to the German *belieben* ("to love"), *Liebe* ("beloved"), and the Latin *libido*.[4]

But during the late seventeenth century, as the meaning of *knowledge* became more theoretical with the separation of the natural sciences from natural theology, the word *belief* was for the first time used to describe intellectual assent to hypothetical—often dubious—propositions. Scientists and philosophers inspired by the sciences were the first to employ *belief* in this sense; but in religious contexts the Latin *credere* and the English *belief* retained their original connotations well into the nineteenth century.

It was Charles Darwin's theory of evolution through the process of natural selection that finally transformed the meaning of *belief* into intellectual assent to a set of propositions established by empirical verification. *Belief* now meant "opinion." In the natural sciences, of course, the ideal is

---

3. Armstrong, *The Case for God*, 81.
4. Ibid., 87.

beliefs publicly established by the rigorous application of scientific methods to the investigation of natural processes that have widespread acceptance in the scientific community cross-culturally. Some of these scientific beliefs posed, and still do pose, serious challenges to some forms of Christian faith. When this happened, as in the case of Christian fundamentalism's interaction with evolutionary biology, Protestant neo-orthodoxy, and conservative strands of Roman Catholicism, the meaning of the word *faith* was rapidly transmuted into belief in a body of theological propositions usually intended as a defense against the challenges of scientific opinion to Christianity's worldview. This process in turn created a fictitious war between science and religion.[5]

Admittedly, many progressive Christians have little, if any, difficulty interrelating their faith with scientific understandings of natural processes. Yet even progressive Christians continue to confuse faith with belief in liberal doctrinal propositions. But as Wilfred Cantwell Smith has noted, *faith* does not mean "belief," in any of the world's cumulative traditions.[6] *Faith*, in all the world's religions, is "trust," "betting one's life on," or as Paul Tillich phrased it, betting one's life on an "ultimate concern." Faith is not belief in or assent to a series of doctrinal ideologies. One *finds* oneself in a state of faith, according to all of humanity's religious ways. We do not argue or believe ourselves *into* a state of faith. We *find* ourselves in a state of faith and then try to interpret (that is, to make sense of) where we find ourselves, which is the purpose of theological reflection. Accordingly, beliefs may be elegant or clumsy, true or false, intelligent or stupid, creative or not. Beliefs may even express faith, as in Anslem's definition of theology as "faith seeking understanding." But beliefs are never, in themselves, faith.

Of course the object of the faith in which one finds oneself is of utmost importance and is not identical in the world's cumulative traditions. Buddhists bet their lives on the historical Buddha's Way of release from suffering and the attainment of Awakening as summarized by the Four Noble Truths: (1) all existence is suffering; (2) the cause of suffering is clinging to permanence, particularly permanent selfhood; (3) release from suffering is possible; and (4) the way to achieve release from suffering by following the Noble Eightfold Path: right viewpoint, right aspiration, right speech, right conduct, right livelihood, right concentration, right effort, and right mindfulness. Faithful Buddhists do not first believe these doctrines and

---

5. See Brooke, *Science and Religion*; Polkinghorne, *Belief in God in an Age of Science*.
6. See W. C. Smith, *Faith and Belief*; and W. C. Smith, *The Faith of Other Men*.

then trust them; faithful Buddhists find themselves aware of the fact of universal suffering because of their own experiential confirmation of suffering, and then follow the Buddha's teachings because it makes existential and intellectual sense for them to do so. Buddhist faith (*śraddhā*) leads to "right viewpoint" and involves the response of the whole person: his or her emotions, intellect, and body in the practice of the Buddha's Way as formulated in the many schools of Buddhist teachings and practices.

Jews bet their lives, often literally, on God's revelation of a way of life embodied in the Torah interpreted through a 2,000-year tradition of rabbinic exegesis. Similarly, Muslims bet their lives on the final revelation of God's will recited to the prophet Mohammed in the seventh century as recorded in the 114 chapters of the Qur'an ("The Recitation") and interpreted in the *Hadith* or "Custom" of the Prophet Mohammed.

Christian faith also has an object. The object of Christian faith is not an anthology of sacred texts called the New Testament but a narrative about a Galilean peasant who lived two thousand years ago named Jesus of Nazareth. In this man's life, death, and resurrection, his followers experienced God "in the flesh"—certainly not all that God is, but nevertheless God. Christians have been betting their lives on the events of this narrative ever since. So while the New Testament bears witness to this narrative, the object of Christian faith cannot be captured in propositions, even in propositions recorded in the New Testament. Yet there is also a hiccup: neither can Christian faith be expressed nonpropositionally or apart from the New Testament. This is why, in the words of Catherine Keller, "theology is one hulking body of truth claims,"[7] which is why I often wonder about which Jesus Christians are talking about.

For the sake of clarity, I shall follow Marcus Borg's lead throughout this book and use the term "pre-Easter Jesus," to mean the historical Jesus as reconstructed by contemporary historical scholarship.[8] In this regard, my particular predilections are informed by the New Testament scholarship of Borg and of John Dominic Crossan, Douglas E. Oakman, and K. C. Hanson.[9] Briefly stated, by the historical Jesus I mean a Galilean peasant born in or near the village of Nazareth between 4 and 6 BCE, who around

---

7. Keller, *On the Mystery*, 20.

8. See chapter 6 for a fuller discussion of the historical Jesus as a Jewish mystic and teacher of a subversive wisdom of living without a why.

9. Borg, *Meeting Jesus Again for the First Time*; and Borg, *The Heart of Christianity*; Crossan, *Jesus*; and Crossan, *The Historical Jesus*; Oakman, *The Political Aims of Jesus*; and Oakman, *Jesus and the Peasants*; and Hanson and Oakman, *Palestine in the Time of Jesus*.

the age of thirty was baptized by John the Baptist. After his baptism, he spent approximately a year traveling in Galilee as an itinerant teacher. He was a mystic who had experienced, probably numerous times, *apophatic* ("negative-way") experiences of union with God as well as *kataphatic* ("affirmative-way") awareness of God's presence in, with, and under all things and events. Such experiences were not unique to Jesus and have occurred for numerous human beings, past and present. Because of his sense of intimate connection with God, Jesus lived and taught from a profound sense of the interdependence of all things and events. He was also a teacher of nonconventional wisdom and a social-political revolutionary.

A band of disciples followed and supported him—a group that possibly included an inner circle of twelve male disciples mentioned in the Gospels but that also included a larger number of male followers and female disciples who played central roles in the Jesus movement. Jesus spent the last week of his life in Jerusalem teaching in and around the temple during Passover. As they had been in Galilee, his teachings about God's preferential option for the poor and those oppressed by the domination systems of his day—the Roman empire, the temple priesthood, and the Herodian rulers of Galilee who ruled in Rome's name—found eager listeners. This angered both the temple priests and the Roman authorities because Jesus's popularity was construed as a rebellion against their authority. Jesus was arrested by the temple leaders, charged with sedition, and handed over to the Roman military governor of Judea, Pontius Pilate, who ordered Jesus's execution by crucifixion around the year 30.

Jesus was baptized by John the Baptist, but went far beyond John's apocalyptic preaching of the imminent reign of God. That is, when Jesus found his own voice, it was squarely within the Israelite and Judean prophetic tradition's call for social and economic justice, which he connected with his own vision of the reign of God. He taught that the kingdom or commonwealth of God is present in the struggle for justice on behalf of the poor and marginalized. For Jesus, justice and compassion were two interdependent sides of the same coin because human beings and God are interdependently connected. God, whom Jesus probably addressed as Abba, is experienced in compassionate and just relationships that constitute the community he called the kingdom of God—a community that is both a present and a future reality that God will ultimately establish in the near future. Finally, Jesus did not refer to himself as Messiah.

By the post-Easter Jesus, I mean the Christ of faith as portrayed in the New Testament, particularly in the four Gospels and the Epistles of the Apostle Paul, the creeds, Christian mystical experience and negative theology, two thousand years of theological reflection and argument, and in the experiences of ordinary Christians. The post-Easter Jesus is a theological interpretation of the pre-Easter Jesus. The pre-Easter Jesus and the post-Easter Jesus are, of course, interdependent, but they are not identical, and both are historical constructions. In the pre-Easter historical Jesus and the post-Easter Christ of faith Christians apprehend God active in history since the first moment of the creation of the universe, as portrayed in the Prologue to the Gospel of John (John 1:1–18).

So as a historian of religion living in the twenty-first century I have gradually found myself in a state of Christian faith that affirms the biblical narratives in which the historical Jesus and the Christ of faith are portrayed as utterly interdependent. I agree with the general Christian claim that in the life, death, and resurrection of the historical Jesus as the Christ of faith human beings have encountered God in the flesh, who is simultaneously incarnated in all things and events at every moment of space–time since the universe's origin at the Big Bang.[10] But I have witnessed the power of creative transformation in all of the world's cumulative religious Ways. What I have witnessed prevents me from universalizing my particular Christian faith and practice as the only way by which human beings can be redeemed (in Saint Paul's, Augustine's, and Martin Luther's language) by God's grace. I have also witnessed too much that is banal, oppressive, and just plain stupid in all the world's cumulative religious traditions to affirm that any religious Way is the only Way. The facts of religious pluralism demand Christian dialogue with the world's cumulative religious traditions and with the natural sciences as the most important imperative for contemporary Christian theological reflection. The traditional Christian imperialism spawned by reducing faith to belief in doctrines is contrary to the Tanakh and the New Testament.

As I have noted in a previous publication, exactly what the Incarnation discloses about God in Christian experience and theological reflection has created enormous cognitive dissonance.[11] For example, classical Christian theology's reflection on the relation between God's impassivity and God's

---

10. By analogy, this is similar to the way an artist incarnates himself or herself into a painting or a musical composition or a sculpture or a poem or novel.

11. See Ingram, *Theological Reflections at the Boundaries*, 14–29.

nature as love has engendered cognitive dissonance from which contemporary theological reflection is still in the process of recovery. The New Testament and Christian theological tradition holds that the fundamental character of God revealed through the Incarnation is best described by the term the historical Jesus used: "compassion" (*ḥesed*), translated into Greek in the New Testament as "love" (*agapē*). But the meaning of the declaration, "God is love" is not always clear in classical Christian theism. We know from our own experiences that love involves sympathetic responsiveness to the persons we love. Sympathy means feeling the feelings of others, grieving over the grief of others, rejoicing with the joys of others. Yet traditional Christian theism posits that God's character is identified not only as love but also as completely impassive, which has created a severe cognitive dissonance that has haunted classical Christian theism since the fourth century: a completely impassive deity without sympathetic response toward the creatures of the world that God is declared to love.

In fact, there was always an awareness that divine impassivity, which originates in Greek philosophy, particularly in Aristotle's *Metaphysics*, was in serious conflict with the New Testament's assertion of God's love for creation. For example, Anselm, living in the eleventh century, asks in one of his prayers, "Although it is better for thee . . . to be compassionate, passionless, than not to be these things; how art thou . . . compassionate and at the same time, passionless?" Anselm tried to resolve this contradiction by concluding, "Thou art compassionate in terms of thy being."[12] That is, God *seems* compassionate *to us*, but is not *really* compassionate.

In the thirteenth century, Thomas Aquinas in the *Summa Theologica* also concluded that love is not part of God's nature: "For in God there are no passions. Now love is a passion. Therefore, love is not in God's nature."[13] Thomas then makes a distinction between two kinds of love: love that involves passion and one that does not. He then concludes, following Aristotle, that God "loves without passion"[14]—similar to the way a skillful physician cures a patient's illness without being affected positively or negatively by the pain the patient suffers. Accordingly, for Anselm, Aquinas, and much subsequent Catholic and Protestant theological reflection, the

---

12. Anselm, *Proslogium*, 11, 13. This is also cited Cobb and Griffin, *Process Theology*, 44–45.

13. Thomas Aquinas, *Summa Theologica* 1, Q, 20. Art 1, obj. 1, cited in Cobb and Griffin, *Process Theology*, 44–45.

14. Thomas Aquinas, *Summa Theologica*, ans. 1, cited in Cobb and Griffin, *Process Theology*, 44–45.

model of God at work is that of a father who has no feeling for his children. God does not feel their experience and needs, and (like any patriarch) loves them in the sense that God dispassionately gives them good things, which is the meaning behind Aquinas's assertion that divine love is a purely outgoing expression of "active good will."

The notion that love is purely impersonal is in serious conflict with the New Testament's, particularly the Gospel narrative's, portrayal of God's compassion as impartially directed to all creation. These same biblical texts contradict classical theism's notion that all persons are not equal in regard to God's loving concern, since the majority of human beings are judged by God (because of original sin) to be worthy of eternal torment. Particularly in traditional Protestant theology, but also Catholic theology, love is defined as "active good will." The idea of sympathetic compassion is simply missing. In fact a contemporary Christian theological treatise on *agapē* portrays love as totally predestined, with no element of responsiveness on God's part to the experiences of the objects of God's love.[15] The implication is that God loves some human beings (a minority of Christians) more than others (the majority of Christians and all non-Christians). In this way, classical theism's notion of divine impassibility undercuts the biblical witness to God's loving compassion and justice. The notion of divine impassibility is also the theological source of traditional Christian imperialism.

Process theology has responded to the cognitive dissonance created by classical theology's assertion of divine impassibility in light of the New Testament's quite clear affirmation that God is actively engaged with the sufferings and joys of the world. The New Testament portrays God as anything but impassive. Process theology is often called "dipolar theology," in contrast to classical theism's assertion of divine impassivity. Charles Hartshorne argued that there are two "poles" or aspects of God's nature: God's unchanging, abstract essence (which eternally constitutes God as God) and God's creative actuality (that aspect of God that is temporal, relative, dependent, and constantly changing because of God's relationships with the world). In each moment of God's experiences there are new and unforeseen happenings, which God can experience and know only as they occur. There is no divine predestination, which means that God's concrete knowledge does not include future events before they occur. God's concrete knowledge of the world is dependent on the decisions made by human and other living

---

15. Nygren, *Agape and Eros*, 77–78.

beings. God's knowledge is always relativized by (in the sense of internally related to) events in the universe as they happen.[16]

Hartshorne's way of describing divine dipolarity was influenced by Alfred North Whitehead's ideas, but is not identical with Whitehead's philosophical vision. Whitehead distinguished between God's primordial nature (what God is eternally as God) and God's consequent nature (what God becomes through God's continual interaction with all entities in the universe at every moment of space–time). God's consequent nature is what God becomes from moment to moment as God compassionately interacts with all things and events. In other words, God is fully actual, receptive, and responsive to the ever changing conditions of human and nonhuman beings. Furthermore, divine relativity is not limited to mere knowledge of events in the universe. Divine relativity is characterized by responsive sympathy not only to human beings but also to all entities in existence. This means that it is not merely the content of God's knowledge that is dependent, but also God's emotional states. Accordingly, God enjoys our enjoyments and suffers with our sufferings.[17] This as it turns out, is exactly the way God is portrayed in the Tanakh and the New Testament.

According to the reality therapy of the Tanakh and the New Testament, life is a process entailing both joy and suffering, with suffering being the primary experience of the vast majority of human beings and other life forms that share existence on planet Earth. To be alive is to suffer. But this is not a fact of existence God decides in advance. There is neither double predestination (found in John Calvin's theology) nor predestination by foreknowledge (found in Luther's theology) anywhere in the Bible. Suffering did not come into creation because of an act of a primal disobedience by the first human beings in the Garden of Eden, supposedly located somewhere in present-day Iraq. The cause of suffering is the Second Law of Thermodynamics and evolution.

Evolution is a process whereby forms of life achieve greater and greater complexity (from the first emergence of organic molecules into single cells in pools of primordial soup about half a billion years ago, to the societies of single cells that constitute forms of life that share this planet today). All forms of life on this planet and anywhere else life in the universe might exist are created by the process of evolution. Evolution is a process by which random mutations are passed on reproductively over time, aiding existing

---

16. Hartshorne, *Divine Relativity*, chaps. 2–3; Hartshorne, *Omnipotence*, chaps. 1–2.
17. Whitehead, *Process and Reality*, 342–51.

species either in adapting to changes in their environments or in evolving into new species capable of adapting to their environments.

Evolutionary processes have led to the emergence of great species diversity and to patterns of natural beauty that can send a poet's heart singing (where beauty is the whole of nature's interdependence that is greater than the sum of its parts). But evolution is also a process that engenders great suffering. What Darwin called "the economy of nature" and "the struggle for existence" not only creates species, but also simultaneously causes their extinction. Life must eat life to be alive, and it is the fate of most species, if not all, to become extinct. But prior to the extinction of a particular species, all of its living members must suffer and die. More species have become extinct then have emerged from the process of evolution.

My point in this brief meditation is that Christian theological reflection on suffering must be contextualized by the biological facts of evolution and what human beings contribute to natural suffering beyond what evolution demands. Natural suffering must be the starting point from which to reflect on human caused suffering, including the suffering the historical Jesus experienced on the cross. Of course all life forms suffer. The existence of natural suffering has nothing to do with human actions and choices, although the depth of natural suffering is often increased by human actions and choices. Natural suffering just is, and it presents a different, though interdependent, theological issue for Christians than does the suffering human beings impose on themselves and on nonhuman life forms. Consequently, from a Christian theological perspective, reflection on suffering requires clarification about the meaning of selfhood as this relates to the concept of sin. But first, a preliminary observation is in order.

Theological reflection on any topic should never be in general, but only in particular (to paraphrase philosopher George Santayana). Accordingly, my reflection on the self and suffering as related to the notion of sin offers a "particular" viewpoint from a Lutheran historian of religions who looks at human experience through the lens of Whiteheadian process philosophy, who grounds his theological reflection in dialogue with the natural sciences, and who practices interreligious dialogue as his primary mode of theological reflection. So I cannot, and do not, claim that what follows represents Christian opinion in general. Indeed, many Christians might find my particular theological reflections troublesome, including many in my own Lutheran community. So while I do not claim that what follows is normative Christian theological reflection, I do claim that it is fully Christian.

Classical Christian teaching on human selfhood originated with Christianity's appropriation of the categories of Greek philosophy, particularly Platonic, Aristotelian, Neoplatonic and Stoic thought. Understood through these philosophical lenses, God creates each human being as an embodied soul, and there exists as many souls as there are human beings. Each human soul is the eternal, unchanging center of each human being's rational, emotional, and moral experiences and functions as the coordinating center of self-identity through time. When a person's body dies, the soul is released from its physical embodiment, its final destiny assigned by God according to its deeds while embodied: paradise, an intermediate state called purgatory (in Roman Catholic theology), or permanent punishment in hell. Of course, Christian tradition offers numerous themes, variations, and levels of complexity and sophistication in teaching about the soul's origins and destiny. These are far more complex and nuanced than what I have described. But all are open to two critiques: (1) they have little, if anything, to do with biblical images of God, and (2) they have little, if any, relation to how persons actually experience (or how God experiences) self-identity through time.

Contemporary biblical scholarship consistently demonstrates the nonduality of biblical images of human selfhood, both in the Tanakh and the New Testament. Nowhere in the Bible do images of human selfhood assume a permanent, substantial soul entity that remains self-identical through time. Rather, biblical images of human selfhood are holistic and processive. Accordingly, the Bible portrays the human self as a unity of soul, body, flesh, and spirit, interdependently constituting the whole person throughout the moments of that person's existence until death.

This unity is exemplified in the Apostle Paul's anthropology, where "soul" (*psychē*) does not designate a substantial soul entity and corresponds to the Tanakh's use of the Hebrew noun *nephesh*, meaning "life," "vitality," and "aliveness." The *psychē* is a particular "life" that can be cared for, saved, judged, or lost. Paul always connected *psychē* with *soma* or "body," which does not denote only a person's physiological or moral attributes but rather the whole person—mentally, morally, and physically. We do not *have* bodies; we *are* bodies animated by life until we die. *Soma* and *psychē* are interdependent.

As living, embodied beings, human selves are capable of interaction with the environing world as subjects of their own thoughts and actions. Ideally, we should be at one with ourselves and with God, so that our thoughts and actions correspond to what we or God wills. But according to Saint Paul, human selves are so estranged from one another and from God that all human selves are at the mercy of "powers" and forces not under our control, but of our own making. Paul named the totality of these "powers" *sarx* ("the flesh"). "Life according to the flesh" leads to a state of existence called "sin." Sin is living our lives as if we are the center of the universe and behaving with self-interest accordingly. The operative word is *egoism*, a condition that Paul thought cannot be overcome by anything human beings do. Consequently, Paul taught that "salvation" (although "redemption" more accurately expresses his understanding) can occur only through God's grace. *Redemption* means the self's redemption from death as the penalty for sin in the form of resurrected embodied life after death, which Paul believed was accomplished through the resurrection of the historical Jesus after his crucifixion.

The point of this brief summation of Paul's anthropology is to underscore that one of the enduring theological discussions that has been ongoing in the history of Christian theological reflection centers on what is called the atonement: on exactly how the death of the historical Jesus overcomes our separation from God, from nature, and from each other, which is the result of sin. Mainline Christian tradition in its plurality of expressions asserts that God's justice must first be satisfied so that universal human sinfulness can be forgiven. According to this theory, God sent his son Jesus into the world as a sacrifice to pay the penalty for sin—death—on behalf of all human kind so that once God's justice is satisfied, God's grace can bring human beings into a relation with God in that state which the New Testament refers to as the "kingdom of God." This interpretation is a substitutionary or ransom theory of the atonement. Substitutionary theories of the atonement have been, in numerous forms, the primary teachings about how the life, death, and resurrection of the historical Jesus are redemptive.

My objection to such theories is that they are theories of divine child abuse, as Christian feminist theologians have long noted, which also lead to Christian oppression of women, non-Christians, nature, and other disadvantaged, minority communities. All are contrary to how the New Testament's portrays God's nature as love interdependent with justice. My particular theological reflection on this matter is rooted in the so-called moral theory of the atonement put forth by Peter Abelard (1079–1142). I have translated the moral theory of the atonement into the categories of Whiteheadian process theology. Abelard taught that God's love, not forensic justice, is at work in the atonement. What he meant was that when human beings apprehend the death of the historical Jesus (either at the actual time of the crucifixion or now in faith two thousand years later), they simultaneously apprehend the love of God incarnated in the world: that is, within rough-and-tumble historical existence. This apprehension, if it happens, occasions repentance, because the crucifixion demonstrates both God's love for all creation (including human beings) and the suffering inflicted on God's love by human sinfulness.

Or reread through the lenses of process theology, God has always been in continual interdependent relationship with all things and events at every moment of space–time, since the beginning of space–time. In this relationship, God supplies an "initial aim" that each occasion of experience achieves the maximum self-fulfillment of which it is capable in interdependent relation to the whole of existence. But every actual occasion also possesses its own "subjective aim" for itself, so that the society of actual occasions of experience that constitute the human self pursues, more often than not, its subjective aim for itself in ways contrary to God's initial aim for the self. The source of human freedom and sin originate here.

The historical Jesus, according to process theology, is fully human. But Jesus, probably because of his apophatic experiences of union with God and his kataphatic experiences of God's presence in the world, conformed his subjective aim for himself to God's initial aim for Jesus, and in so doing became *the* Christ. One can therefore say that Christ in the form of God's initial aim is incarnated in all things and events at every moment of space–time, past, present, and future. But the historical Jesus became *the* Christ because he identified his subjective aim for his own self-fulfillment with God's initial aim for the historical Jesus. Or as Jesus is reported to have said shortly before he was killed, "Not my will but your will." Thus, Jesus was not different from other human beings; or in the language of the Nicene Creed, "he was made man." But in the unity of his subjective aim with God's will (God's initial aim), he was in harmony with the Christ or *logos* incarnated in all things and events—at least according to the Prologue to the Gospel of John.

So I follow Abelard's lead, but again reinterpret Abelard through Whiteheadian process theology. My reflection on Jesus's crucifixion in relation to what I have learned from the natural sciences has taught me two things, First, I have learned to look at suffering wherever it occurs—in me, in other human beings, in other living nonhuman beings, and in God's experiences of creation: here trips and hunches and moans God; here sputters the living, breathing tortured-to-death historical Jesus. I deeply believe that this points human beings to the fundamental character of existence: from great suffering something other than suffering emerges that is redemptive. In other words: "It is not Jesus' death that transforms, but his life—a life of embodied love that had the power to persist beyond death as the stories of the resurrection mysteriously suggest."[18] The second thing I have learned is that pain and suffering, even if redeemed by God, is still pain and suffering, which is always planted in me and in every other living thing caught in the field of space–time. Pain and suffering happen not because God wills it, but because suffering is ingredient within the evolutionary processes of life itself.

Of course the mystery that is the resurrection has almost been ruined by dogmatic assertions. But for those having ears to hear, Christian faith is a Way of life that will engender sacrifices of various kinds, sometimes in the face of terrifying oppressive power. But sacrifice, even Jesus's death on the cross, is never the purpose of Christian faith. Sacrifice is the risk of faith. But it was not the death of the historical Jesus that transformed his followers, but his life. As Keller writes, "No more than Jesus did Gandhi, King, or Romero *want* or *seek* to die. Even when they could predict their imminent death, as each seems to have done, they were not choosing to die but to *persist in love*."[19]

This is the point of entry into the difficult path of Christian theological reflection: to persist in love working for justice for all human beings and, I think, for every life form that lives on planet Earth and anywhere else life might have evolved in the universe. Love and justice are so interdependent that one cannot be experienced without the other; one cannot work for one apart from the other. Justice is the communal expression of love. The difficult path of Christian faith requires following the Way the historical Jesus taught within the ever shifting contexts of history. Everything else— theological doctrines, moral codes, participation in a church community,

---

18. See Keller, *On the Mystery*, 122–23.
19. Ibid., 123.

dialogue with the world's religions and the natural sciences—is, while essential for bringing understanding into Christian faith as Anselm argued, of secondary importance. This is why Christian theological reflection needs to pay more attention to the "Negative Way" (*via negativa*) of Christian mysticism as well as the mystical Ways of non-Christian traditions. I more fully examine this proposition in the following chapters. While Christian faith may not be difficult because, as Luther thought, it comes to human beings through God's grace alone, theological reflection on the meaning of faith, as the Luther and all mystics knew, remains always a difficult path.

FOIUR

What's in a Name?

As a historian of religions, I have witnessed the process of creative transformation at work in every religious Way I have studied. But I have also witnessed much that is stupid, violent, and just plain silly that blocks creative transformation. Both experiences have convinced me that no single religious Way possesses the absolute truth about the Sacred, however named. Two encounters with Buddhists will illustrate what I mean.

Entering into dialogue with persons living faithfully in the depths of a religious tradition other than one's own often clarifies the faith and practice of one's own tradition. Because such persons have heard the lyrics and the music of their religious faith, the authenticity of what they say and do can help Christians hear more deeply the music and lyrics of Christian faith. Such faithful non-Christians are what the paleontologist Loren Eisley called "hidden teachers." Non-Christian hidden teachers, however we run into them, are forms of the grace that envelops everything in this universe, from subatomic particles to ourselves.

In the summer of 2001, I encountered an elderly Zen Buddhist monk in Japan who told me a story. I was one of a number of persons invited to give a lecture at a weeklong conference on a Buddhist text called the *Lotus Sutra*, which is the most widely revered Buddhist text in East Asia. At conferences, I often tire of the scholarly abstractions of academics trying to impress one another, so I played hooky for a day and explored the small town that was the site of our meeting. In the foothills north of town I found a small Zen Buddhist temple and literally ran into a monk on his way to rake a dry garden. He must have been in his eighties, but he seemed to possess more energy and liveliness than any person I have ever met. We talked for a while as he raked the white sand in the dry garden into intricate patterns and explained what I already knew from research on Zen, but in a less abstract way: that Zen gardens are objects of meditation. Each word the abbot uttered seemed to me to harmonize with the rhythm of his raking movements, which were focused and exact. I had never met a man so fully concentrated and aware of his surroundings.

When he had finished raking, he stopped talking and headed back to the small room where he lived in deliberate simplicity. Although he did not verbally ask me to tag along, I knew he had wordlessly invited me to his room for afternoon tea. We entered a rather small, elegantly simple square room with no furniture other than three meditation cushions and a black lacquer writing table in the center, facing a small alcove called the *tokonoma* or "place of honor." Traditionally, a *tokonoma* is a place where guests are seated on cushions on a floor covered with rice straw mats in traditional Japanese homes and in Buddhist monasteries. Usually, a flower arrangement or a hanging scroll or both decorates the place of honor, and honored guests sit with their backs to the hanging scroll and the flower arrangement.

The monk, whose name was Moriya, was supposedly in retirement, although at that time he was training twenty novice monks and a small group of lay Buddhists. When we entered his quarters, he motioned me to sit in front of the *tokonoma*, which had a wonderful flower arrangement he had created that morning, and a seven-hundred-year-old hanging scroll with calligraphy that read, "thundering silence." Thomas Merton, who was a Trappist monk, wrote much of "entering the silence," and it seemed that was what the monk and I had done. Then out of the silence he told me this story:

> *Mukushi, mukashi*, or once upon a time, he began, a Zen master was sitting in *zazen* (seated meditation) when a loud voice broke the silence.
>
> "My name is Tanaka," the voice said loudly. "Please give this to Ueda Roshii and tell him Tanaka is here to see him."
>
> Shortly afterward, a monk entered the Roshi's room, grinning from ear to ear as he handed an *omeishi* (business card) to Ueda Roshi and said, "Mr. Tanaka is here to see you."
>
> The Roshi's eyes narrowed into an angry stare because Mr. Tanaka's *omeshi* was covered with black Chinese characters and Japanese script on both sides, listing all his college degrees, honorary degrees, ranks and titles, board memberships, and so forth. Had there been any more calligraphy, the card would have looked like a small black lacquer chip.

"Tell that worthless bag of bones," the Roshi said angrily, "I don't know who he is. If he doesn't leave the temple immediately, I'll call the police and have his worthless self thrown in jail for trespassing."

The monk flashed another ear-to-ear grin, bowed, left the room, and shut the sliding rice-paper door after him. A few seconds later, the monk said, "Ueda Roshi says you're a worthless bag of bones and he doesn't know who you are. If you do not leave the temple immediately, he'll call the police and have your worthless self thrown in jail for trespassing."

Then the card's owner said, "*dame da na*," which means something like, "I'm such an idiot," followed by, "*wasuremashita*," which means "I forgot." "Please return my business card." Then another silence. "Please tell the Roshi that Tanaka asks to see him."

The monk reentered the Roshi's room and handed him the business card. All the titles, honors, and degrees were crossed out with a ballpoint pen and the only word left was "Tanaka."

Then the Roshi said, "Ah, my old friend Tanaka. Please show him in."

According to the monk, the Roshi and Tanaka had been friends for fifty years, ever since their student days at Kyoto University, where the Roshi had received a doctorate in comparative religions and Mr. Tanaka had received a master's degree in political science.

This story taught me something about the subversive wisdom that the historical Jesus (whose parables and aphorisms have a Zen quality about them) tried to teach his disciples—that the conventional wisdom that celebrates honor and social standing is not wisdom at all, but an illusion. Hearing this story from a elderly, wise Zen monk was for me an experience of what process theologians call creative transformation, an example of "living without a why," as Marguerite Porete put it in the thirteenth century, an example of what Protestant theology names grace.

My second encounter occurred during the same conference on the *Lotus Sutra*, which was hosted by Risshō Kōsei Kai.[1] The conference attendees were invited to a Sunday morning service at a local Risshō Kōsei Kai *kyōkai*, or church. The congregation was seated in neat, straight rows

---

1. "Society for the Establishment of Righteousness and Friendly Interchange." Risshō Kōsei Kai is one of the "New Religions" derived from Nichiren's (1222–82) interpretation of the Lotus Sutra that was founded as a lay Buddhist movement in 1938 by Naganuma Myōkō (1889–1957) and Niwano Nikkyō (1906–1999) to spread the teachings of the *Lotus Sutra*.

on *tatami* mats separated by an aisle, while we as visitors sat in chairs in the rear. The service began when the minister, dressed in a black robe, entered as a group of young people processed down the aisle singing hymns praising the *Lotus Sutra*. (Many Japanese Buddhist lay groups picked up the Protestant flavor of this service from missionaries in the nineteenth century.)

Prior to his sermon, the minister invited a middle-aged woman to give her testimony. She tearfully recounted the conditions of her life prior to her conversion to Buddhism because of the influence of Risshō Kōsei Kai missionaries in her neighborhood: her experiences of physical and emotional abuse by her husband, her long years of drug addiction, her rejection by her children and relatives, her life of poverty as a prostitute. But after she converted to Buddhism, she said, her "negative karma was turned into positive karma": her husband no longer abuses her, she recovered from drug addiction, her children and family now love her, and she no longer engaged in prostitution to make financial ends meet for her family. In other words, this woman blamed herself for her own abuse.

But then in a long sermon in Japanese, so did the minister. As I sat listening to his rather sharp condemnation of the woman's life before she became a member of Risshō Kōsei Kai, reconfirming the woman's blame for her own abuse, I whispered to my friend Mark Unno, "Am I hearing this correctly?"

Mark, who is a Pure Land Buddhist and an important scholar of Buddhist tradition, whispered, "Yes! Shut up!"

After the service ended, we were invited to meet the minister for tea and pastries. Mark went directly to the minister and dressed him down for using Buddhism in such a patriarchal and sexist manner to condemn a very troubled woman whose husband and the other men in her life had so wrongly abused her. "She was not responsible for her abuse," he told the minister.

According to my worldview, while the testimony of this woman might have been a story of her experience of creative transformation, I also witnessed the power of creative transformation in the prophetic words and actions of a Buddhist scholar and friend. Christian tradition has too often been a source of oppression, blaming women for the abuse received from male clergy and from laymen. Sadly, sexism is rampant in all the world's religious traditions.

It is positive and negative experiences such as these that have convinced me of the truth of theological pluralism. Pluralist theologies that emphasize dialogue with the world's religions are often accused of debilitating relativism. But the essential difference between theological pluralism and debilitating relativism is that pluralism is based on the principle that there exists an absolute truth—even as, more often than not, boundary questions arise that force theologians and Buddhist philosophers to employ languages of unsaying to communicate what this reality might be. This is, I suppose, one of the lessons of mysticism cross-culturally. So values exist, and theologians and philosophers can and must say no to certain systems and ideas, particularly to fundamentalist absolutisms of any kind and to any form of sexism. Theological pluralists affirm absolute values but have come to know their limits. Like a Zen koan or the experience of nonsaying that Christian mystics encounter in contemplative prayer, theological pluralism recognizes its own limitations.

More to the point, the term *pluralism* describes the religious experiences and insights recorded in the Tanakh, the New Testament, the Qur'an—indeed in the scriptures of all the world's religious Ways. For far from regarding revelation as fixed and unchanging, Jews, Christians, and Muslims all knew that revealed truth was symbolic, so that scripture should never be interpreted literally, that sacred texts had multiple meanings that could lead to entirely new insights. Revelation is not an event that happened once and for all "delivered to the saints" in the distant past but is an ongoing process, a creative process of transformation that requires human response and ingenuity.

So Jewish, Christian, and Muslim mystics understood that revelation does not provide human beings with infallible information about God (or, in Buddhist terms, Emptying; or, in Hindu terms, Brahman; or the Dao in Chinese religions), because God—however named—is beyond our capacities to understand fully. This seems to me a scriptural foundation for theological pluralism. For specifically Christian theological reflection, the word *God* is elusive. Thus, Jewish, Christian, and Muslim sages, theologians, and teachers insisted on the importance of intellectual integrity and of thinking for oneself in place of clinging nervously to insights and past teachings and doctrines. Such teachers expected people to be inventive, fearless, and confident in their interpretation of faith. So Martin Luther did not so much invent the priesthood of all believers as inherit it.

This is why I agree with the Christian mystics that God is elusively beyond the categories of theological reflection. But just because nothing we say or write literally applies to God does not imply that nothing meaningful can be said or written about God as experienced by human beings. After all, even mystics talked and wrote about God the way poets talk and write about love—in languages of unsaying that is nevertheless language. So the more deeply I reflect on the process of creative transformation that I think is at work in humanity's collective religious Ways, as well as in the universe in general since the Big Bang 13.7 billion years ago, the more I am convinced that Alfred North Whitehead's model of God is, as Luther wrote in his *Small Catechism*, "most certainly true," because it provides a coherent vision for understanding the process of creative transformation at work in the pluralism of humanity's religious Ways.

Translating Whitehead's conception of God into my history-of-religions research program, the Sacred is the source of order and novelty in the universe, to which the particular cumulative traditions of the world's religious Ways refer according to their own distinctive worldviews, named differently by each religious Way. Some religious Ways emphasize (i.e., *prehend*) the Sacred as nonpersonal and ineffable (beyond the ability of language—definitions, doctrines, symbols—to fully comprehend): the ineffability of Brahman in Upanishadic Hinduism or Emptying in Mahayana Buddhism or the Dao (the Way) in Daoist tradition or God in Christian apophatic mysticism. Included in these examples are other mystical traditions such as Islamic Sufism and Jewish Kabbalah. Participants in these Ways seek to experience the connection between themselves and the Sacred, nonpersonally transcendent to, yet immanent within, all finite things and events, through such disciplines as yoga and various forms of meditation and contemplative prayer.

But the vast majority of human beings *prehend* (that is, experience) the Sacred through a range of specific deities. At least judging from the evidence of the Paleolithic cave paintings preserved in the Grotto of Lascaux and elsewhere in France, experience of the Sacred as a personal deity or collection of deities with whom one is in relationship is probably the most archaic form of religious experience. Yet no one has ever encountered the Sacred in general, but only in particular: always bounded by historically and culturally situated images and symbols. Just as there are different ways of being human and participating in history, so too there are different ways of experiencing the Sacred as nonpersonal or personal.

WHAT'S IN A NAME?

Christians encounter the sacred as personal through the four Gospel narrative accounts of the life, teachings, death, and resurrection of the historical Jesus confessed to be the Christ. Faithful Christians trust these narratives as pointers to the relationship between human beings and God the Father, and to the Father's continuing work through the Holy Spirit. In other words, the historical Jesus is apprehended as a lens through which God's relation to the universe is revealed. Similarly, Jews in faith bet their lives on Yahweh's gift of the Torah ("Instructions") and the resulting covenant between Jews and God mediated by Moses on Mount Sinai. Muslims surrender their wills (*'islām*) to Allah as recited by the Prophet Mohamed in the Qur'an, wherein Muslims believe is recorded the "straight way" of humanity's most complete religion. In Hindu devotional faith, the Sacred named Brahman is experienced through as many incarnations or *avatars* ("descents") as you please: Siva, Vishnu, Kali, Krishna, Rama, and a host of other incarnations. Mahayana Buddhists, probably the majority, encounter the Sacred as the Dharma beyond name and form, yet masked by a multiplicity of Bodhisattvas that are objects of devotion. Native people encounter the Sacred personified in natural forces like wind, rain, mountains, lakes, rivers, sun, moon, stars, and the natural forces of growth and decay.

Even so, there is always something nonpersonal about personalized forms of the Sacred as deities. It's not that deities often interact with human beings nonpersonally. (Jesus is reported to have said like rain, God's love for all of creation is disinterested.) The point is that images of deities also reveal that the Sacred is infinitely beyond the scope of human understanding and cultural and historical perspective. Yet, as we learn from both theistic and nontheistic religious Ways, merely because we cannot know *everything* about the Sacred does not mean that we cannot know *something*, since according to the Whiteheadian version of religious pluralism I have described, the Sacred is always interacting with the particulars of the universe as the source of ordered novelty wherever novelty occurs.[2] Included in these particulars are the religious Ways of humanity.

Writing as a Christian theologian, I understand that the Sacred—however named—is the Ultimate Mystery and ineffable boundary generating the cognitive dissonance inherent in all theological reflection.[3] All religious Ways reflect the Sacred according to their own distinctive ways. But none

---

2. For a more fully developed discussion of the experience of the sacred as nonpersonal and personal, see Ingram, *Wrestling with the Ox*, 76–86.

3. See Ingram, *Theological Reflections at the Boundaries*, 51.

can own the Sacred or can claim absolute truth about the Sacred. The Sacred, however named, is not only ineffable but also radically pluralistic. So too is all of reality, as Whitehead argued. Theological pluralism tells us that there exists no one that can be imposed on the many; nor can the many be imposed on the one. Despite the similarities shared by humanity's religious Ways, there will always be one and many, which means that there will exist differences and disagreements about the one Sacred Reality named differently in the plurality of the many Ways of humanity.

Accordingly, that theological pluralism does not allow for universal religious systems like Christianity, Judaism, Islam, Buddhism, or Hinduism seems like a revelation of the nature of the Sacred itself. No model of theological pluralism, including the one described in this book, should be understood as a universal system. Rather, models of theological pluralism are hermeneutical devices for exploring the religious Ways of humanity. So viewed from a Whiteheadian perspective, the Sacred that Christians name God as revealed in the life, death, and resurrection of the historical Jesus as the Christ does not exhaust what God is. No religious Way has a market on the truth about the Sacred.

The similarities in doctrines, teachings, and experiences engendered by meditative and contemplative practices, or the common ethical principles that cut across boundaries of specific religious traditions, are widely known by historians of religions and acknowledged by progressive theologians. Even so, there are important differences between the religious Ways of humanity—some of which are incommensurable and nonnegotiable—that define the unique character of each religious Way. For example, Christian experience and teaching about the Incarnation is not something that Christians can compromise and still coherently participate in a Christian faith community. Likewise, Islamic monotheism is a call not to reduce God to that which cannot be God and surrender to it, which means that no Muslim can accept the Christian doctrine of the Incarnation and remain within the House of Islam. Buddhist nontheism and Jewish, Christian, and Islamic monotheism are incommensurable. What Zen Buddhists mean by *awakening* is not identical with what Luther meant by *redemption*.

The list goes on. But one need not assume that similar experiences and doctrines that seem to cut across religious boundaries possess more evidentiary value for supporting theological pluralism than the nonnegotiables that separate humanity's religious Ways. In this regard, several points require clarification. First, incommensurable teachings, practices, and experiences need not always imply contradiction. Often the differences between religious persons and the communities they represent are complementary. For example, Buddhist practices are thoroughly grounded in a nontheistic worldview. Yet Christian experiences of God as personal also include experiences of God as nonpersonal, as in, for example, Christian mystical theology and practice. Likewise Buddhist nontheism includes elements of devotional practice and experience that seem in many ways structurally similar to Christian theistic experience—elements exemplified by Japanese Pure Land Buddhism.[4] While I as a Lutheran think the Incarnation points to how God has always interacted with the universe, and continues working, the Incarnation of God in the historical Jesus does not exhaust the reality of God, which means that the faith and practices of non-Christians can teach me lesions I need to learn.

Second, the fact that the religious Ways of humanity are quite often incommensurable should surprise no one. If I am right, the religious Ways of humanity are best understood as limited, historically and culturally conditioned means by which human beings have grasped and been grasped by the Sacred, however it is named. According to most of these religious Ways, the Sacred is ineffable Mystery that can be glimpsed and experienced contextually within the pluralism of human culture and history, but only partially and incompletely. Still, just because the Sacred cannot be known completely or expressed in any final way does not mean that human beings cannot say or know something about the Sacred.

Finally, incommensurable teachings and practices are often radically contradictory. This is illustrated by comparing Buddhist nontheism and Jewish, Christian, and Islamic monotheism. For Muslims surrendering to the Qur'an's call not to reduce God to that which cannot be God, the Christian doctrines of the Incarnation and the Trinity can only seem like "idolatry" (*shirk*). Christians, who apprehend God incarnated in the life and death of the historical Jesus, must be in disagreement with Islamic teaching that the historical Jesus, while an extraordinary prophet, can never be a redeemer. In such instances, either both teachings are false or one is true and the other an illusion. But how does one decide, given the fact that religious persons faithful to their tradition's Way can only engage other traditions from the standpoint of their own particular Way? Human beings seem unable to be faithfully religious in general, but only in particular.

---

4. See Ingram, *The Dharma of Faith*.

In reflecting on this difficult issue, it helps to remember that theological pluralism need not lead to the conclusion that all religious doctrines and practices are equally true, or that all religious Ways are equally creative and transformative. For example, concluding that terrorist acts justified by Islamic or Christian distortions about the meaning of the Qur'an or the Bible are not authentic expressions of Islamic or Christian faith and practice is an easy decision. But deciding whether Buddhist nontheism or Christian monotheism, for example, is a true description of the Sacred is quite another matter. While it is reasonable to argue that the religious Ways of humanity are pointers to a common reference, it is not reasonable to conclude that all are equally true, or that one Way is truer than all other Ways. No one possesses enough information to justify this sort of religious imperialism. We may affirm for example, that a particular doctrine or practice of a religious Way is true *for us*. But we cannot do so for anyone else. Or restated in terms of my particular Christian theology, theological pluralism is confessional and therefore should be grounded in the practice of interreligious dialogue.

A further point requires clarification. Christian theological pluralism also requires dialogue with the natural sciences.[5] In the present postmodern age, all religious persons must live out the implications of faith within the context of what the natural sciences are revealing about the physical processes at play in the universe. What the natural sciences are uncovering about these physical processes both challenges and, when approached with care and sensitivity, deepens religious faith and practice in all religious Ways. So according to the Whiteheadian perspective assumed in this and in the remaining chapters of this book, my conclusion is that the Sacred is in, with, and under the universe's unfolding and enfolding natural processes, holding all together in a unity supporting an incredibly amazing pluralism. Some of this pluralism includes religious Ways of humanity.

---

5. As I have argued in Ingram, *Buddhist–Christian Dialogue in an Age of Science*, chap. 6.

FIVE

Butterfly in a Mirror

WHEN LOOKING AT A smudged mirror, the viewer sees the glass. But if the mirror is polished and clear, a visual shift occurs. The glass becomes invisible and only the viewer's self-image is reflected. Vision becomes self-vision. Buddhists and Sufi mystics are fond of the polished mirror as a symbol of the shift of apprehension beyond the distinction of subject and object, self and other, self and world—a shift that they report occurs in apophatic mystical experience. The polished mirror also occurs in Marguerite Porete's *Mirror of Simple Souls*[1] and serves as one of her primary metaphors describing her apprehension of the reality she named God—an ultimate reality beyond the conventional linguistic distinctions of subject and object, self and world, and, in her mystical theology, self and God. Polish the mind's mirror, remove the smudge of linguistically constructed dualities, and what remains is reality as self-vision.[2]

A well-known Daoist symbol of reality as self-vision is Zuangzi's butterfly dream.[3] Once Zuangzi dreamt he was a butterfly fluttering from flower to flower, happy and doing as he pleased. Suddenly, Zuangzi was jolted into a state between waking consciousness and deep sleep and didn't know if he was Zuangzi, who had just dreamt he was a butterfly, or if he was now a butterfly dreaming he was Zuangzi. Reality, "the way things really are," which Zuangzi named the Dao, has a trickster-like character similar to the transformation of a caterpillar into butterfly. Both Zuangzi and his

---

1. All quotations cited from Porete, *The Mirror of Simple Souls*, hereafter cited as *Mirror*.

2. Sells, *The Mystical Languages of Unsaying*, 63.

3. Cf. Watson, *The Complete Works of Chuang Tzu*, 49; and Graham, *Chuang Tzu*, 61.

butterfly are forms of self-transformation. Every thing and event in the universe is a self-transformation of the Dao that is beyond names and forms. What Marguerite and Zuangzi tell us is that the reality they experienced and wrote about transcends linguistic construction.

Here is how Saint Augustine expressed his own experience of unsaying:

> Have we spoken or announced anything worthy of God? Rather I feel that I have done nothing but wish to speak: If I have spoken, I have not said what I wish to say. Whence do I know this, except because God is ineffable? If what I said were ineffable, it would not be said. And for this reason God should not be said to be ineffable, for when this is said something is said. And a contradiction in terms is created, since if that is ineffable which cannot be spoken, then that is not ineffable which can be called ineffable. The contradiction is to be passed over in silence rather than resolved verbally. For God, although nothing worthy may be spoken of him, has accepted the tribute of human voice and wished us to take joy in praising him with our words.[4]

Unlike Saint Augustine (so perhaps foolishly), I am not willing to silently to pass over the paradoxes of mystical discourse even though I agree that they cannot be resolved. If they could, theologians and philosophers could get on with their jobs with the aplomb of bricklayers. Certainly mystics do not silently pass over the linguistic paradoxes engendered by their talk about an ineffable ultimate reality.

What is going on here? To confront this question, I shall place Zuangzi's butterfly in Marguerite Porete's mirror, since my working thesis in this chapter is that the structure of their respective mystical discourses reflect similar, if not identical experiences of apophatic "union" in spite of the differing cultural and religious contexts of their discourses. But first I offer again a brief summary of the nature of mystical discourse.

It is not possible to completely distinguish between mystical experience and mystical theology, or between mystical experiences and their theological or philosophical interpretations in any absolute way. For in most cases, mystical theory precedes and guides the mystic's whole way of life and directs his or her practice (*praxis*). Theory—that is, theology, and, in non-Western traditions of mysticism, philosophy—"is not some form of epiphenomenon, a shell that can be peeled off to reveal the real

---

4. Augustine, *On Christian Doctrine*, bk. 1, ch. 6, 10–11.

thing."[5] Accordingly, while I argued in the previous chapter that apophatic experiences are characterized by a common structure cross-culturally, I do not argue that all mystical experiences are identical, since part of a mystic's experience is the *preparation undergone before the experience occurs* and *the interpretation of the experience after it occurs*. But given the common neurological structures of the human brain and central nervous system that have been evolving among *homo sapiens* for thirty-five to forty thousand years, it can be reasonably argued even on biological grounds that apophatic experiences exhibit a common structure that is not culturally or religiously specific, even as *how* mystics interpret the meaning of these experiences *is* culturally and religiously specific.

Recognizing the interdependence of experience and interpretation means that historians of religions and theologians need to understand mysticism contextually so that mystical *texts* are the primary objects of study. If this is so, then about what do historians of religions and theologians reflect when they reflect on mysticism? In place of a straightforward answer to this question, I want to offer three conclusions in process about the generic features of mysticism.

First, mysticism is an element of the religious traditions of which they are a part. No mystic has ever practiced something solely called mysticism. Mystics practiced Christianity, Judaism, Islam, Buddhism, Hinduism, or Daoism.

Second, the term *mysticism* names a particular religious process. Although the goal of mystical theory and practice may be conceived as a particular kind of encounter between God and human beings, or between Infinite Spirit and finite human spirit, "everything that leads up to and prepares the mystic for the encounter, as well as all that flows or is supposed to flow from it afterwards for the life of the mystic, is also mystical even in a secondary sense."[6]

Third, mysticism is an attempt to experience and express direct consciousness of the presence of God (in theistic religious traditions) or of a nonpersonal ultimate reality (in nontheistic religious traditions). In this regard, mysticism and shamanism are structurally experiential cousins.[7] Sometimes this presence is expressed as union or oneness. Sometimes mystical experience is not a matter of union. For most mystics the direct

---

5. McGinn, *Foundations of Mysticism*, xiii–xiv.
6. Ibid., xvi.
7. Craffert, *The Life of a Galilean Shaman*, chaps. 5–7.

experience of God's presence does not involve ontological union with God and is referred to as kataphatic mysticism.

So the mystical elements of a religious tradition are part of its teachings and practices, and concern the preparation *for*, consciousness *of*, and reaction *to* the immediate or direct presence of God in Christianity, Judaism, Islam, or theistic forms of Hinduism; or in nontheistic traditions, of union with Brahman in Advaita Vedanta, the experience of Awakening in Buddhism, or union with the Dao in Daoist tradition.[8]

Finally, mysticism as a religious phenomenon is as pluralistic as the religious traditions that house mystical practices and experiences. Yet there is one thing that is not specific to one tradition, about which all actual mystics seem to agree: mystical experience, especially apophatic experience, defies verbalization and conceptualization because it is utterly empty of content. Accordingly, it can only be publicly presented indirectly, poetically, by a series of verbal strategies in which language is used not so much informationally as transformationally; that is, not to convey content but to assist hearers or readers to hope for or to achieve a similar experience of contentless consciousness.

Accordingly, I shall assume as axiomatic that the paradoxes, aporias, and coincidences of opposites within apophatic mystical discourse—whatever their cultural and religious context—are not merely apparent contradictions. These contradictions and paradoxes are real, but not irrational, illogical, or incoherent. For the apophatic mystical writer, the logical rule of noncontradiction functions for object entities. But when the subject of discourse is a non-object and a no-thing, it is not illogical when the logical rules of ordinary discourse are suspended.

Certainly, mystical discourse is not the only discourse that cannot directly name its object. For example, the reason many mystics choose poetry for their mode of expression has to do with the ways poetry subverts ordinary discursive language. Both poets and mystics overcome the limits of discursive language because poetry, drama, or most any art form risks being trivialized when its meaning is defined or paraphrased discursively, as anyone knows who needs to have the humor of a joke explained. Or as Michael Sells notes, "Apophatic texts have suffered in a particularly acute manner from the urge to paraphrase the meaning in non-apophatic

---

8. Ibid.

language or to fill in the open referent—to say what the text really meant to say, but didn't."⁹

What, then, can be said of the apophatic discourse of Marguerite Porete and Zuangzi? How are we to understand relationship between Marguerite Porete's mirror and Zuangzi's butterfly?

Marguerite Porete's Mirror

Marguerite Porete was burned at the stake on June 1, 1310, at the Place de la Grève in Paris.¹⁰ She was from Hainaut in northern France and was a member of a group of religious women known as the Beguines, whose social status was somewhere between laity and clergy. In part, the Beguines modeled their rule after the recognized monastic orders, which were mainly Dominican where she lived, but they were free to leave their communities and marry.

Marguerite Porete belongs to a distinguished line of thirteenth-century Beguine mystical writers that included Mechthild of Magdeburg and Hadewijch of Antwerp. She had written a book—*The Mirror of Simple Souls*—that was condemned and burned in her presence at Valenciennes by Guy II, bishop of Cambria, in 1306. She was later accused of circulating the *Mirror* after its condemnation and was brought before Guy's successor, Philippe of Marigny, who turned her over to the inquisitor of Haute Loraine. Eventually, she was handed over to the Dominican inquisitor of Paris, Guillaume Humbert.

Marguerite refused to cooperate with the proceedings against her, to testify, or to take the formal oath required of persons charged with heresy. So without her testimony, Humbert submitted a list of articles from the *Mirror* to twenty-one regents of the University of Paris, who declared fifteen articles heretical. A panel of canon lawyers then handed her over to the provost of Paris to be burned along with a converted Jew who was charged with relapse. In 1309, Guiard de Cressonessart, who called himself the Angel of Philadelphia, intervened on Marguerite's behalf, and he too was arrested and ordered to renounce his teachings. Unlike Marguerite, the Angel of Philadelphia recanted and was condemned to life imprisonment.

---

9. Sells, *The Mystical Languages of Unsaying*, 3–4.

10. For more detailed biographical information, see: Brunn and Epiney-Burgard, *Women Mystics in Medieval Europe*.

Within a few years of her burning,[11] Marguerite's name was associated with a movement called "the heresy of the free spirit," and her *Mirror* influenced the development of Meister Eckhart's mystical theology. Portions of Eckhart's sermons were condemned as heretical for reasons similar to those that had led to Marguerite's condemnation. Unlike Marguerite, however, Eckhart was not arrested, tortured, or burned at the stake.[12]

Marguerite wrote the *Mirror* as a dramatic allegory in which five characters—Lady Love (Dame Amour),[13] Annihilated Soul (L'Ame Anneantie), Reason (Raison), FarNear (Loingprès) and High Courtesy (Pure Courtoise)—engage in an extended discussion about love and theology. The text brings together the apophatic paradoxes of mystical union and the troubadour tradition of courtly love into a mystical language of rapture. The result is an apophasis of desire.

The high point of the drama occurs when Reason, who symbolizes the Aristotelian epistemology of the Scholastic schools and their theologians, is so perplexed by the paradoxes of Lady Love that he dies. The context of dialogue that leads to Reason's death is a seven-tiered cosmos of mystical stations, the fifth and sixth of which are the center of interest, with the seventh station being beyond all words and associated by Lady Love with the afterlife.

Early in the *Mirror*, Marguerite describes the "simple" soul as a soul in union with God, a soul whose will is annihilated by God's love. Such a soul (1) is saved by faith without works, (2) exists only in love, (3) does nothing for God, (4) leaves nothing for God to do, (5) can be taught nothing, (6) is a soul from whom nothing can be taken and to whom nothing can be given,

---

11. Marguerite's trial, condemnation, and execution was, according to Bernard McGinn, "a critical moment in the history of Christian mysticism, one equivalent to the execution of Al Hallaj in the story of Islamic mysticism . . . Marguerite is the first documented case of an execution for mystical heresy in Western Christianity. Unfortunately, it was not to be the last. Her death was not just an individual tragedy; it also provided critical ammunition for an ongoing struggle between the mystical and the institutional elements of Christianity that has continued almost down to the present day" (McGinn, *The Flowering of Mysticism*, 244).

12. For a discussion of Marguerite's influence on Meister Eckhart's mystical theology, see McGinn, "Meister Eckhart and the Beguines in the Contest of Vernacular Theology"; Lichtmann, "Marguerite Porete and Meister Eckhart"; Hollywood, "Suffering Transformed"; and Sells, "The Pseudo-Woman and the Meister."

13. Her name for God, a reference to 1 John 4:8—"Whoever does not love does not know God, for God is love" (NRSV).

and (7) has no will.[14] Each of these traits of the soul deliberately provokes Reason and questions the medieval Church's understanding of the way of salvation. The doctrines and practices of what Marguerite calls "Holy Church the Little" (the sacramental system of fourteenth-century Roman Catholicism) can be superseded only by the shock to Reason that Marguerite's description of the liberated soul in union with God entails. Reason, jolted into attention, is driven to demand from Lady Love an explanation.

Lady Love then describes a seven-stage process whereby the soul is led to union with God.[15] These stages include the ascetic, churchly, and contemplative practices advocated by the majority of fourteenth-century religious and semireligious persons. In her description of the lower stages, Marguerite rejects the forms of ascetic, ecstatic, and mystical piety particularly associated with women.[16] For the soul, she writes, must pass through seven stages, each initiated by God's grace, and each marked by three deaths: the death of sin, the death of nature, and the death of the spirit. Subsequent to each death are two stages, one characterized by complacency and the other by a sense of dissatisfaction that leads to the next death.

The soul enters stage 1 after the initial death to sin, at which point the soul is given divine grace, is freed from mortal sin, and begins to follow the twofold commandment to love God and the soul's neighbor. When this minimal Christian life seems inadequate, the soul is drawn into stage 2. Here, the soul abandons all riches and honors in order to follow the evangelical counsel of perfection, of which Christ is the example. This initiates the soul's death to nature and leads to stage 3. Now the soul possesses an abundance of love and desires to do good works. This paradoxically leads the soul to give up all external works in order to be capable of greater love for God. This is the life of contemplation, ascetic piety, poverty, fasts, prayers, devotions, and martyrdoms—in other words, monasticism.

Marguerite thought that most Church authorities were stuck at stage 3. These she described as "lost souls" stuck in "Holy Church the Little." Lost souls, according to her, are incapable of attaining freedom because they refuse to see that asceticism, contemplation, and spiritual delight do not represent the soul's highest perfection. Such practices—based on self-willed works—merely serve to absent the soul from God. But rather than taking the divine absence as an intrinsic part of union with God, lost

---

14. Porete, *Mirror*, 82–83.
15. The most detailed description of these stages is found in chap. 118 of the *Mirror*.
16. Hollywood, *The Soul as Virgin Wife*, 97–103.

souls attempt to elicit experiences of divine sweetness through suffering, asceticism, and internal contemplative works. Such souls, she says, are like "merchants" who believe that they can barter with God.

Some souls, however, are drawn to stage 4, where the first steps toward simplicity are experienced. The soul is now bewildered. But although still "merchants" and "servants" and still possessed of will and works, souls at this stage are no longer lost because they recognize that bewilderment is better than nothing. This recognition leads to renunciation of the will, which is stage 5. Here, the soul recognizes its previous self-deceptions. Such recognition, in turn, engenders fleeting experiences of the utter and complete transparency of the soul in its union with God. This marks the death of the spirit, which is twofold, involving both the death of reason and the death of will. This experience pushes the soul into stage 6: union with God. Union with God is completed at stage 7, when the soul departs the body at death to be permanently in union with God. This is a stage beyond description, of which the soul catches imperfect glimpses at stage 6.

Two ingredients of this framework of spiritual progress are important to understand. The first ingredient is Marguerite's description of three kinds of death. These three kinds of death are transitions that give birth successively to three higher forms of life as they move the soul toward spiritual perfection. Death to sin gives birth to the life of grace in stage 1. Here, one begins with the commandments of the church and the help of God, who commands that one love God with all of one's strength, mind, and heart and one's neighbor as one's self. The life of grace is the life of ordinary believers. Death to nature gives birth to the life of the spirit, meaning the attempt to follow the counsels of evangelical perfection. This is life lived in obedience guided by reason. Death to the spirit gives birth to the divine life. The spirit must die because it is filled with will. Even though will in the life of the spirit is spiritual, it is still will. The death of the spirit and the departure of will in stage 5 are absolutely necessary for the birth of stage 6. All rudiments of the soul's own will must be annihilated by the divine will, which then, at stage 6, becomes the soul's will. In this state the soul wills nothing, because God's will wills the willing of the annihilated soul. That is, between the soul's will—we might say *self* in contemporary speech—and God's will or self *there exists no ontological duality*. Or in Marguerite's language, what takes place at stage 6 is an "exchange of wills,"[17] which Sells describes as an "apophasis of desire." Sells writes:

---

17. Porete, *Mirror*, 166.

The apophasis of desire includes the admonition to give nature all that it desires, but that admonition applies to the annihilated soul in which nature and will and spirit have died. After the death of the will, the soul no longer needs to work contrary to her will because the soul is no longer the doer or the worker, but rather the deity works in her.[18]

The second ingredient of Marguerite's framework is her description of the state of the annihilated soul. According to her, in union with God's will, the soul shrinks into a smallness so great that it can no longer find itself because it has "fallen" into the certainty of knowing nothing and willing nothing. So the soul is freed of desire, and will is disencumbered of all things and has no care for anything, including self, neighbors, or God. Having no desires and having abandoned all self-will, the soul reverts to a "pre-created state" of being, or in Marguerite's language, to what the soul "was when she was not." Liberated from its will, the soul has no *why*, and acts "without a why" and "without a what." Again in Marguerite's words,

> This is right, says Love, for her will is ours. She has crossed the Red Sea, her enemies have been drowned in it. Her pleasure is our will, through the purity of the unity of the will of the Deity where we have enclosed her. Her will is ours, for she has fallen from grace into the perfection of the work of the Virtues, and from the Virtues into Love, and from Love into Nothingness, and from Nothingness into clarification by God, who sees Himself with the eyes of His Majesty, who in this point has clarified her with Himself. And she is so dissolved in Him that she sees neither herself nor Him, and thus He sees completely Himself alone, by His divine goodness . . . Now He possesses [the will] without a why in the same way that He possessed it before she was and made a lady by it. There is no one except Him; no one loves except Him, for no one is except Him, and thus He alone loves completely, and sees Himself completely alone, and praises completely alone by His being Himself.[19]

In addition, Reason also dies because living without a why involves letting go of the distinctions by which Reason (conventional Scholastic theology) functions. Union entails complete abandonment, of will, works, reason, and self-vulnerability. Thus union with God can occur only in the context of absolute trust, or faith. All defenses and desires for security are

18. Sells, "The Pseudo-Woman and the Meister," 114.
19. Porete, *Mirror*, 167.

gone, and the soul, annihilated in loving union with God, no longer exists in the formal sense as a subject that wills and acts in relation to an object. The only will and action are the will and action of God, so that the annihilated soul is like a mirror free of the smudge of egoistic self-effort in which the soul is a self-reflection of God's will.

I might also add that Marguerite's mystical theology ends up with a Luther-like conclusion. The apophasis of desire that occurs in the state of union engenders in the *Mirror* a radical reconception of love, of God as love, and of the authentic Christian life as that which involves acts or "works" that are ends in themselves.[20] Any act done to achieve something from God that one thinks one does not have is a "work" that engenders enslavement of the will: living according to conventional ethical virtues, participating in the sacraments, practicing monastic contemplative disciplines. All these are the required activities for participation in "Holy Church the Little."

Although Marguerite's teaching that the liberated soul is beyond the sacraments of the institutional church of her day is not a conclusion that Luther would have supported, her understanding of salvation by grace through faith rather than by works (in her words "living without a why") is pushed in her mystical thought to an extreme point that would have pleased Luther: the soul that gives up all will and works is no longer concerned with poverty or riches, honor or dishonor, heaven or hell, self and other, self and deity. In such a state of selfless abandonment of will and reason, one "lives without a why," without the calculation that life in the Church required of persons at stages 1 to 4. Such a state of utter selflessness, of annihilation of the will and of reason (both of which are concerned with works), cannot be achieved through any sort of self-effort. It only occurs when the soul is "ravished" by the grace of its divine lover. Or in Marguerite's words, when

---

20. See Luther on union with Christ in *Freedom of A Christian* in *Martin Luther*, 60–61. For Luther, union with Christ involved an "exchange of characteristics." In Luther's words, "Accordingly, the believing soul can boast of and glory in whatever Christ has as though it were its own, and whatever the soul has Christ claims as his own . . . The soul is full of sins, death, and damnation. Now let faith come between them and sins, death, and damnation will be Christ's, while grace, life, and salvation will be the soul's." Of course the exchange of characteristics that occurs between the faithful Christian and Christ in the union of faith did not presuppose that the soul experienced any sort of ontological union with Christ. Christ and the faithful soul in a state of grace always remain ontologically distinct in Luther's theology. Nor would Luther have concluded that the reception of God's "grace through faith alone" occurred because of any human action, including the achievement of a mystical experience of union with God. For Luther, apophatic and kataphatic experiences are not caused by human self-effort but by God's grace.

"the One in whom she is does His work through her, for the sake of which she is entirely freed by the witness of God Himself... who is the worker of this work to the profit of this soul who no longer has within her any work."[21]

Without self-will, God's will and love flow into and out of the liberated soul and accomplishes what it accomplishes, so that "I do not owe [God] any work since He Himself works in me. If I should place my own [work] there, I destroy His work."[22] In other words, because the liberated soul's own will is annihilated in and by God's love, the soul in union with God leads a life of "actionless-action" reminiscent of what Daoist tradition and the Zuangzi describe as *wu-wei*.

Zuangzi's Butterfly

Marguerite Porete was a historical person. But it is not clear that there existed a historical Zuangzi. The "seven inner chapters" of the *Zuangzi*—the earliest part of the entire text—is an anthology of various sayings most probably representing a school of philosophical Daoism that is somewhat different from that preserved in the *Dao De Ching*. Like the sage Laozi, the figure of Zuangzi may be a composite caricature of a whole school. Furthermore, no original text of the seven inner chapters has been discovered, and the history we have of the transmission of the text is very unclear. If the generally accepted dates of the Inner Chapters are accurate (between 350 and 275 BCE, which are also the generally accepted dates of the *Dao De Ching* [*Classic on the Way and Its Power*]), then the Daoist mysticism personified by the *Zuangzi* evolved in one of the most creative periods of the evolution of Chinese religion and philosophy.

The *aporia* or "irresolvable dilemma" of the *Zuangzi*'s worldview is similar to what one finds in the *Dao De Ching*: the Dao (the ultimate reality that underlies, creates, and glues together all things and events in the universe at every moment of space–time—past, present, and future—is characterized as both nameless and nameable:

> The Way that can be told of is not the Unvarying Way:
> The names that can be named are not unvarying names.
> It was from the Nameless that Heaven and Earth sprang:
> The named is but the mother that rears the ten thousand

---

21. Porete, *Mirror*, 121.
22. Ibid.

creatures each after its kind.[23]

Or as the *Zuangzi* formulated the *Dao De Ching*'s discourse about the irresolvable dilemma,

> The Way has its reality and its signs but is without action or form. You can hand it down but you cannot receive it; you can get it but you cannot see it. It is its own source, its own root. Before Heaven and Earth existed it was there, firm from ancient times. It gave spirituality to the spirits and to [the gods];[24] it gave birth to Heaven and Earth. It exists beyond the highest point, and yet you cannot call it lofty; it exists beneath the limit of the six directions, and yet you cannot call it deep. It was born before Heaven and Earth, and yet you cannot say it has been there for long; it is earlier than the earliest time, and yet you cannot call it old.[25]

The technical terms of the apophatic language of this text, referred to as Zuangzi's "willow words," need to be unlocked. First, the unnameable Dao names the total process of becoming. In other words, the Dao is an unnameable ultimate reality, not as a single universal order, but as the totality of all possible orders of things and events that have occurred, are occurring, or can occur in the universe. Furthermore, because each existing thing and event in the universe is an element of the Dao's totality, each possesses its own *de* ("power" or "virtue"). *De* denotes the Dao as it exists particularly in individual things and events. Thus *de* points to a thing's or an event's intrinsic excellence as a particular expression of the Dao, and in this sense constitutes the nature of a thing or event that simultaneously defines both its actuality (what it is) and its potential (what it can become).

The concepts of Dao and *de* form a third concept, *dao de*, which Watson thinks is best understood as the relation between a "field" (Dao) and its "focus" (*de*), a relationship that can be imagined through the model of a holograph. In a holographic image, each element contains all other elements and all elements contain every single element. Like a holograph, every thing and event in nature in accordance with its own individual nature (*de*) mirrors the totality of nature (the Dao). Likewise, the totality of all possible

---

23. Waley, *The Way and Its Power*, 141.

24. Watson used "God" in his translation of this passage and gives a misleading monotheistic implication that is historically not evident in traditional Chinese conceptions of deity. Therefore, I have substituted "gods" for "God."

25. Watson, *The Complete Works of Chuang Tzu*, 81.

things and events that constitute nature (the Dao) is reflected in the nature of every single thing and event's particular nature, that is, in its *de*.

Given the *dao de* structure of nature, the meaning of the concepts *wu chih*, *wu wei*, and *wu yü* can be easily grasped. *Wu chih*, or "no knowledge," involves knowing the *de* of things and events as mirror reflections of the Dao rather than knowing a thing or event in relation to some abstract philosophical category (as, say, an instance of a universal or a member of a class). As the *Dao De Ching* puts it,

> Banish wisdom, discard knowledge,
> And the people will be benefited a hundredfold.
> Banish human kindness, discard morality,
> And the people will be dutiful and compassionate.
> Banish skill, discard profit,
> thieves and robbers will disappear.[26]

As the *Zuangzi* explains it,

> The True Man of ancient times knew nothing of loving life, knew nothing of hating death. He emerged without delight; he went back without a fuss. He came briskly; he went briskly, and that was all. He didn't forget where he began; he didn't try to find out where he would end. He received everything and took pleasure in it; he forgot about it and handed it back again. This is what I call not using the mind to repel the Way, not using man to help out Heaven . . . Therefore, he who delights in bringing success to things is not a sage; he who has affections is not benevolent; he who looks for the right time is not a worthy man; he who cannot encompass both profit and loss is not a gentleman; he who thinks of conduct and fame and misleads himself is not a man of breeding; he who destroys himself and is without truth is not a user of merit.[27]

Accordingly, *wu chih* is knowledge of the *dao de* relationship of each thing and event in nature that engenders an understanding of nature that focuses on the *de* of each thing and event as a particular form of the Dao.

Wu-wei or "actionless action" or "non-ego assertive action" is action in accord with and expressive of unprincipled knowing. The essential character of such action is that it is not guided by abstract rules or calculating

---

26. Waley, *The Way and Its Power*, 238.
27. Watson, *The Complete Works of Chuang Tzu*, 78.

principles. Actionless-action is illustrated by some advice Zuangzi is said to have given his friend Hui Tsu about how to deal with a "useless" tree:

> Maybe you've never seen a wildcat or a weasel. It crouches down and hides, watching for something to come along. It leaps and races east and west, not hesitating to go high or low until it falls into the trap and dies in the net. Then again there's the yak, big as a cloud covering the sky. It certainly knows how to be big, though it doesn't know how to catch rats. Now you have this big tree and you're distressed because it's useless. Why don't you plant it in Not Even Anything Village, or the field of the Broad and Boundless, relax and do nothing by its side, or lie down for a free and easy sleep under it? Axes will never shorten its life, nothing can harm it. If there's no use, how can it come to grief or pain?[28]

Finally, *wu yü* means something like the "absence of desires" or "non-attachment to the fruits of action." "Actionless action" (*wu wei*) is "action without desire for or attachment to the fruits of action" (*wu yü*). Another way of characterizing this concept is as "objectless action," in the sense that one may act in accord with the Dao and enjoy and reap enjoyment without demanding that one define, possess, or control the object of one's enjoyment. Thus, "the Perfect Man has no self; the Holy Man has no merit; the Sage has no fame."[29]

The meanings of all these technical terms come together in the concept of *tsu jan*, meaning something like the "self-creativity" ingredient in all things and events as reflective, like a mirror of the Dao. *Tsu jan* is a Daoist "categorical imperative" with the following ethical implication: act in accordance with your *de* or nature as a reflection of the Dao in ways that express "actionless action" and "the absence of attachments."

Clearly, these Daoist conceptions, as they function in the *Zuangzi*, imply an understanding of reality as an unnameable order in which we are enjoined to be "spontaneous" (*tzu jan*) in the practice of "actionless action" (*wu wei*) in balanced harmony with the forces of *yin* and *yang* by deferring to the natural and intrinsic excellence (*de*) of every thing and event we encounter in the natural order, and by enjoying similar acts of deference directed toward us by virtue of another's appreciation of our *de*. In this sense, Daoist practice is really an aesthetic that shuns antecedent principles or abstract norms in a manner similar to the way a creative individual would

28. Ibid., 35.
29. Ibid., 32.

refuse to depend on past norms for the determination of present actions. Daoist creativity thus engenders the spontaneous (*tzu jan*) production of novelty.

Above all, there can be, in Zuangzi's view, no rules external to the creative processes of nature. Occasionally, however, human beings can model these spontaneous, creative natural processes. That is, like a butterfly, the Daoist sage seeks not to transform the natural order to achieve human ends. Rather, the sage cooperates with the natural order to achieve the Dao's ends. Without ego, as a mirror-like self-reflection of the Dao, the sage lives "without a why" (as Marguerite would have phrased it in her theological world), in accord with nature. In other words, the Dao's action in nature replaces the sage's ego so that the sage's ego does and wills nothing. Accordingly, Zuangzi's advice runs as follows:

> Do not be an embroiderer of fame; do not be a storehouse of schemes; do not be an undertaker of projects; do not be a proprietor of wisdom. Embody to the fullest what has no end and wander where there is no trail. Hold on to all that you have received from Heaven but do not think you have gotten anything. Be empty, that is all. The Perfect Man uses his mind like a mirror going after nothing, welcoming nothing, responding but not storing. Therefore he can win over things and not hurt himself.[30]

Some Concluding Observations

It is clear that the experience of mystical union to which Marguerite's and the *Zuangzi's* respective languages of unsaying point occurs within thirteenth-century Christian theological tradition and fourth-century-BCE Daoist tradition respectively. But it is equally clear that neither Marguerite's Christian theological tradition nor the *Zuangzi's* Daoist philosophical tradition created the unitive mystical experiences to which their respective languages of unsaying point; further, the unitive experience to which their respective languages of unsaying point cannot be reduced to their theological and philosophical traditions.

Additionally, the language of unsaying employed by Marguerite and the *Zuangzi* constitutes cross-cultural evidence that apophatic experiences

---

30. Ibid., 97.

of union are absolutely contentless. Consider, for example, the following accounts from the *Mirror* and the *Zuangzi*. Marguerite writes:

> Now this soul, says Love, has her right name from the nothingness in which she rests. And since she is nothing, she is concerned about nothing, neither about her self, nor about her neighbors, not even about God Himself. For she is so small that she cannot be found, and every created thing is so far from her that she cannot feel it. And God is so great that she can comprehend nothing of Him. On account of such nothingness she has fallen into the certainty of knowing nothing and the certainty of willing nothing. And this nothingness of which we speak, says Love, gives her the All, and no one can possess it in any other way . . . If she does any exterior thing, it is always without herself. If God does His work in her, it is by Him in her, without herself, for her sake . . . For she has nothing of herself. She has given all freely without a why.[31]

Compare Marguerite's description of "living without a why" to the *Zuangzi*'s description of living naturally according to "actionless action," free from "attachments." This way of living results from the sage's union with the Dao (of which the sage's life is a self-reflection). Union with the Dao is an experiential encounter in which

> the Great Way is not named; Great Discriminations are not spoken; Great Benevolence is not benevolent; Great Modesty is not humble; Great Daring does not attack. If the Way is made clear, it is not the Way. If discriminations are put into words, they do not suffice. If benevolence has a constant object, it cannot be universal. If modesty is fastidious, it cannot be trusted. If daring attacks, it cannot be complete. These five are all round, but they tend toward the square. Therefore understanding that rests in what it does not understand is the finest. Who can understand discriminations that are not spoken, the Way that is not a way?[32]

In other words, Marguerite's *Mirror* and Zuangzi's butterfly are evidence that during unitive mystical experience there occurs no sensory experience and no emotional experience. Further, unitive mystical experience provides no intellectual content upon which to reflect for its duration, because sensation, emotion, or reflection would create the subject–object duality structure of ordinary experience. Additionally, for the duration of

---

31. Porete, *Mirror*, 156–57.
32. Watson, *The Complete Works of Chuang Tzu*, 44.

a unitive mystical experience beyond the subject–object duality, there does not seem to exist an awareness that one is having such an experience, since this awareness too would create the subject–object duality structure of ordinary experience. Literally, during an apophatic experience, there occurs a duration, usually rather short in time, of objectless and contentless pure consciousness. In this mental state, consciousness appears to reverberate at the impact of an ontological reality that lies beyond while simultaneously deep within the mystic's awareness. But the mystic's meaning is misinterpreted if we think this reality is beyond or outside the mind. When knower and known are united, that union does not allow any distance for subject–object oppositions such as those that structure ordinary conscious experience. In apophatic mystical experience, the mystic's mind functions in a mode of "being with reality" rather than "reflecting upon reality."[33]

Accordingly, if we are to give credence to the *Mirror's* unsaying testimony, in mystical union, Marguerite's consciousness was turned from self-consciousness to God-consciousness, where her mind became both a center of God's presence and God's absence. This seems confirmed by her need to empty her mind of all conscious content before the final state of union. With a mind emptied of content, God *becomes* her mind's content and God's will *becomes* her will, so that one in union with God acts in the world "without a why" in a way similar to what the *Zuangzi* would recognize as "actionless-action." For Marguerite, God was experienced as the ultimate dimension within the finite, inaccessible within the accessible.

So too for Zuangzi. In union with the Dao, one is turned from self-consciousness to Dao-consciousness. With a mind emptied of its own content, the Dao becomes the mind's content, at which point one's willful ego disappears so that one's actions in the world are the Dao's action. That is, the Dao is apprehended as the ultimate dimension of the finite, accessible within the inaccessible. So one is enabled to act "without acting," that is, "without a why." For the *Zuangzi*, mystical union is an ontological union with the Dao; for Marguerite, mystical union is interpreted as union with God's will.

Accordingly, while apophatic mystical experiences seem structurally identical, because the common biological structures of the human brain seem similar cross-culturally, the ways in which mystics talk about their experiences are not similar cross-culturally. This can be illustrated by the ways Marguerite Porete and the *Zuangzi* employed different languages of

---

33. Idel and McGinn, eds., *Mystical Union*, 10–11.

unsaying to interpret the meaning of their particular apophatic experiences. Interpretation is always a constructive part of both apophatic and kataphatic mystical experiences.

This means that mystical experience never proves anything other than that one is having a mystical experience. This holds true for both apophatic and kataphatic mystical experiences. While mystics in every religious Way are driven to countercultural and oftentimes severely nonconventional relationships with conventional and institutionalized religious traditions, all mystics remain grounded in the traditions that train them. This means that before mystical experiences occur, mystics are trained by the languages of their particular religious traditions about what they should look for before and after their experiences. There is no such thing as noninterpreted nonmystical or mystical experience. Christian, Buddhist, Hindu, and Muslim mystics described and wrote about the meaning of their experiences as Christians, Buddhists, Hindus, and Muslims. In other words, they all unconventionally engaged in the difficult path of theological or philosophical reflection. Christian theologians need to listen to and appropriate through dialogue these collective languages of unsaying.

SIX

A Theological Reflection on Mystical Experience

WE ARE ALL SKEPTICS now, believers and unbelievers alike. In our contemporary postmodern world marked by religious pluralism, there is no one true faith evident at all times and in all places. Every religious tradition is one among many. The clear lines of orthodoxy in every religious Way are made crooked by human experience, are complicated by human lives. Everywhere, believers and unbelievers are in the same predicament, thrown back onto themselves in complex circumstances, looking for a sign. As ever, religious beliefs make claims somewhere between revelation and projection, somewhere between holiness and human frailty. But the relation between faith and belief for so long upheld by the plurality of human societies is now back on the individual, where it belongs. And if this is the case, individuals need to pay attention to the mystics that inhabit all religious Ways, who in their particular and often peculiar ways model a life of grace whose structure of existence Marguerite Porete characterized as "living without a why."

Of course, not all religious experiences are mystical experiences. Attending services in a church or synagogue or mosque or temple may occasionally induce intellectually and spiritually meaningful religious experiences, but these are not usually mystical experiences. This is not to say that conventional religious participation may not sometimes engender mystical experiences, or that conventional religious practices cannot open us to a life of grace. Mystical experiences may also occur apart from any participation in a religious tradition, often generated by a deep experience of the beauty and interconnectedness of nature. More often than not, mystical experiences occur apart from the practice of disciplines like meditation or contemplative prayer, although such disciplines may prepare one for attaining a mystical experience. That is, the practice of meditation and contemplative prayer of itself does not always (in fact, does not often) lead to the achievement of mystical experiences.

So if the testimony of the mystics cross-culturally is to be believed, something like grace is a primary element in mystical awareness because it feels like a gift. Furthermore, experiencing a kataphatic or apophatic experience is not necessarily better or more profound than what people sometimes experience on Sunday morning sitting in church listening to a good sermon, participating in a liturgy, or kneeling before an altar to receive the Eucharist. Mystics themselves in every religious Way did not view their experiences as superior to those of the majority of ordinary faithful persons. Mystics also knew that those who have mystical experiences often suffer from delusion, particularly when mystics absolutize the meaning of what they experience by surrounding it with rigid doctrinal interpretations. Mystical experiences of themselves are not proof of anything corresponding to reality. So when judging the truth value of a mystic's experience or his or her interpretation of the implications of such an experience, we must be "wise as serpents." The history of religions is replete with persons selling mystical snake oil. The only epistemological test is pragmatic: as the historical Jesus is reported as having said, "you know them by their fruits."

Since I so strongly agree with Marcus Borg's claim that the historical Jesus was a Galilean mystic, as were the eighth-, seventh-, and sixth-century Israelite and Judean prophets whose prophecies are preserved in the Tanakh; and since mystical experiences lie at the heart of humanity's religious Ways generally, I shall devote this chapter to a fuller explanation of mystical theology. But I want to be clear: while I think that mystical experiences are the origin experiences that gave birth to humanity's religious Ways, I do not claim that mystical experiences are the only forms of valid religious experience. Most human beings are not mystics, although it can be argued that persons living at the depth of their faith have occasionally experienced something like a mystical experience. So it is probable that numerous human beings have had experiences that fall under the descriptive category of mysticism. Most often, such experiences are not the result of specific training in disciplines of meditation, and are unexpected even as they are related to the external circumstances of a person's life. They also mostly fall under the category of kataphatic, but not always. The following is a personal example.

A THEOLOGICAL REFLECTION ON MYSTICAL EXPERIENCE

During my university's spring break in 1999, my wife, Regina, and I drove from Tacoma, Washington, to Joshua Tree, California, to visit my father because we needed some "road time" to get away from the business of university teaching and from my wife's work as a medical social worker. On the first day, we drove south on Interstate 5 to Redding, California, where we stopped for the night. When I called my father to let him know about our progress, he kidded me about turning sixty-five the week before.

"How does it feel to be an old man?" he laughed.

"You think sixty-five is bad," I retorted. "How does it feel to have a sixty-five-year-old kid?"

I could hear the pride in his voice. "Not bad at all."

"We should arrive at your place early tomorrow evening."

"Great. Watch the traffic through LA."

When we pulled into his driveway the next day at 7:30 p.m., I noticed that the curtains were drawn over the windows. I rang the doorbell, but the only sound in the house was the continuous barking of his small dog. I also tried all the doors and windows. All were locked tight. That's when I knew something was terribly wrong, because my father had been expecting us and would not have left his house without leaving a note on the front door. So I called the San Bernardino County Sherriff. When a deputy arrived, I explained the situation to him, and he broke into the house through a back window. It was dark by then, and I could see his flashlight moving throughout the house. Finally, he opened the front door and told me that my father was lying dead on his bed. "I'm sorry," the deputy said. "It looks like he died in his sleep, but this will have to be confirmed."

"I understand," I said.

As the paramedics were removing my father's body, I called my two brothers and told them our father was dead. The next day they and their wives met us at Dad's house, and we began the weeklong process of taking care of his affairs—and grieving.

I was fairly calm through it all—until the day of the funeral. I was scheduled to deliver a homily celebrating his life. As I gazed at his open coffin before the service began, I felt suddenly overwhelmed by grief and turned away and ran out of the chapel. I don't remember how far I had gone, but it seemed that out of nowhere I felt a calming presence flow over and through me that stopped me in my tracks. All my surroundings were ordinary but seemed different, and I saw them with a newness that comes with the experience of seeing something clearly for the first time:

the trees moved by a soft wind, the topaz blue Southern California sky, the gray cemetery headstones, the deep green grass, the coolness of the breeze flowing over my skin, soft as a kiss. Everything seemed so interrelated and interdependent, so much so that not even death could sever my father from my life. And the sense of deep peace that enveloped me like a quilt was something I had not experienced before.

My wife saw me run out the chapel door and followed me. "Are you okay?" she softly asked when she caught up with me.

"Yes," I said, as I took her hand and walked back into the chapel.

Spring break was coming to a close, and life must move on to be alive. So we left for Tacoma the day after my father's funeral. In the morning two days later, as I was in that intermediate state between deep sleep and wakefulness, I felt a presence enfolding itself around me the way my father used to hug me when I was a child whenever I felt sad or anxious about something. It didn't last very long, and I woke up and began getting ready for another day of teaching and faculty committee meetings.

To this day I do not know what to make of these experiences. I certainly do not see them as proof that the Christian teaching of resurrection corresponds to reality, or that an experience of my father's presence after his death proves anything. Most neuroscientists would explain these experiences as the result of biochemical processes going on in my brain initiated by grief over my father's death. But scientific materialism of this sort explains away, rather than explaining what I experienced. All I know is that while I cannot prove that what I experienced corresponds to anything external to the biological process involved in my mental and emotional state of mind at the time, I also cannot prove that they do not. So I prefer living in the ambiguity of the possibility that the universe is much wilder and more open to processes than either natural scientists or theologians can at present comprehend. But I do maintain that I experienced what Michael Sells calls "the dilemma of transcendence."[1]

According to Sells, any discourse on mysticism begins with an *aporia*, an "unresolvable dilemma of transcendence." By definition, the transcendent is ineffable, and therefore beyond names. But in order to claim that the transcendent is beyond names, it must be given a name (i.e., "the transcendent"). So any statement of ineffability—"X is beyond names"—generates the *aporia* that the subject of this statement must be named as "X" in order

---

1. Sells, *The Mystical Languages of Unsaying*, 1–2.

A THEOLOGICAL REFLECTION ON MYSTICAL EXPERIENCE

to affirm that it is beyond names as "X." All mystics cross-culturally have experienced the dilemma of transcendence.

To restate this in the language of Christian mystical theology, what we call God is literally not God. As Paul Tillich liked to say, God is beyond "God." One of the great temptations in the history of Christian theology is to mistake the infinite for the finite names we give it. And of course, every religious Way has its own mystical traditions, whose words cover over its own distinctive idolatries. But mystics swim in experiential insight that negates (or as contemporary theologians say, "deconstructs") the absolutisms that presumes to name God like some person or entity, to know God with certainty, either abstractly or literally. That is, doctrine and dogmas are effectively submerged; they are present but are not the point. This is how mystics "keep theology on the way."[2]

So there are three possible responses to the dilemma of unsaying. The first is remaining silent, not talking about it, for a whole range of reasons: no one can or would understand what I'm talking about; my friends might think I'm crazy; an experience no words can describe might lead to actions that most conventional people would judge to be strange; or I simply want to hold on to the experience in the depths of privacy.

The second response involves trying to distinguish the ways the transcendent is beyond names from the ways it is not. For example, in medieval Christian theology, it was common to make a distinction between two kinds of naming: (1) naming "God-as-God-is-in-God's self," and (2) naming "God-as-God-is-for creatures" Or another way was the distinction between the "incommunicable deity-as-it-is-in itself" and the "deity-as-it-is-in human minds."

A third response begins with a refusal to resolve an *aporia* dilemma by means of a distinction between two kinds of names. That is, the dilemma is accepted as a genuine *aporia*: that is, as irresolvable. But this acceptance, rather than leading to silence, leads to a distinctive mode of theological discourse called "negative theology" (*via negativa*) in Christian tradition. Negative theology is most generally associated with Christian apophatic mysticism, as exemplified by Marguerite Porete, Meister Eckhart, or John of the Cross. Negative theology also occurs in non-Christian traditions and is exemplified by the author of the seven inner chapters of the *Zuangzi*, or by the explanations of numerous Zen masters about the nature of *satori* in the *Hegigan-roku* ("Blue Cliff Records"). My point is that even negative

2. Keller, *On the Mystery*, 19.

theology is always a reflection of the religious Ways in which particular mystics have been trained. Neither apophatic nor kataphatic experiences occur in general but only in particular. They are never uninterpreted experiences, because there exists no such thing as an uninterpreted experience.

So mystical discourse is negative in the sense that it denies that the transcendent can be either named or given attributes. The denial that the transcendent can be named must in some sense be valid, as every poet knows; otherwise ineffability would not be an issue. Insofar as it is valid, however, a formal declaration of ineffability turns back on itself and undoes itself, also as every poet knows. So to declare that "X is beyond names" entails that it cannot be named "X." But the statement "it cannot be named X" is also suspicious, since "it," as a pronoun, substitutes for a name. But the transcendent is beyond names. So the moment we try to describe the *aporia* of transcendence, we are caught in a linguistic infinite regress that twists against itself like a Möbius strip.

Accordingly, any statement mystical theologians make—either positive or negative—reveals itself in need of correction by an opposite statement even as an opposite correcting statement must itself be corrected, *ad infinitum*. The transcendent subject of theological discourse continually slips back beyond every effort to name it and every effort to deny its nameability. It is this infinite regress that provides the energy of mystical discourse. This is why the negative theologians of Judaism, Christianity, and Islam did not stop naming God: the infinity of the Sacred generates an endless multiplicity of possible names, as exemplified by the "Ninety-nine Beautiful Names of God" in the Qur'an.

According to Paul Mommaers and Jan van Bragt, "mysticism is primarily a matter of consciousness."[3] Something previously unknown suddenly flashes into consciousness. Mystics are also social beings, which means that they do not slip into a private language to talk about what they have experienced. Their narratives of unsaying are rooted in plain English, French, Spanish, Latin, Greek, Japanese, Chinese, Hindi, and so forth. This means that mystics are grounded in the religious traditions of their culture's worldview and religious Ways. Furthermore, mystics try to convey in ordinary language not only the content of their experiences but also its force and objectivity, and in so doing they make truth claims about what the Sacred is and is not. But mostly, they claim to simply know by experience what is there for anyone to know according to their particular religious

---

3. Mommaers and van Bragt, *Mysticism, Buddhist and Christian*, 12.

Way. In other words, they employ the languages, practices, doctrines, and concepts of the religious Ways in which they find themselves. So while, structurally, apophatic mystical experience is universally characterized by nondual union with the Sacred (an experience in which the mystic's sense of utter separateness from the object of experience drops away from consciousness, so that that mystical union is not mediated by the mystic's own consciousness), nevertheless, after the mystic returns to normal subject-object awareness, his or her discourse reflects the religious Ways in which he or she participates, but unconventionally. Experience and interpretation of experience are always part of both apophatic and kataphatic mystical experiences. This is amply illustrated by contemporary Buddhist–Christian interior dialogue.

Buddhist–Christian Interior Dialogue

The relation of mystical experience to the specificity of the particular religious Ways in which mystics find themselves may be illustrated by a brief comparison of Buddhist and Christian mystical experience and discourse. From a rather abstract theoretical standpoint, the Buddhist and Christian Ways seem to be polar opposites: Buddhism as a religion of Awakening and Christianity as a religion of faith, conventionally understood as belief in doctrines; Buddhism as a religion of experience versus Christianity as a religion of theological reflection; Buddhism as a religion of wisdom versus Christianity as a religion of love; Buddhism as a religion of equanimity and introversion versus Christianity as a religion of desire and extroversion; Buddhism centered on the human self versus Christianity centered on God. But these dualisms have been shown to be no more than false stereotypes by a type of contemporary Buddhist–Christian dialogue that has its origins in the monastic dialogues Thomas Merton began in 1968, now referred to as "interior dialogue."[4] For Buddhists and Christians engaged in interior dialogue a rather surprising reality has emerged where mystical experience plays a central role. As Merton explained it,

> A little experience of such [contemplative] dialogue shows at once that this is precisely the most fruitful and most rewarding level of ecumenical exchange. While on the level of philosophical and doctrinal formulations there may be tremendous obstacles

---

4. See Merton, "Monastic Experience and East-West Dialogue." See also Mitchell and Wiseman, *The Gethsemani Encounter*.

to meet, it is often possible to come to a very frank, simple, and totally satisfying understanding in comparing notes on the contemplative life, its disciplines, its vagaries, and its rewards.[5]

The question is, how does interior dialogue transcend doctrinal differences between Buddhism and Christianity without, on the one hand, rejecting the specific qualities of each or, on the other hand, making Buddhist and Christian doctrines mere abstractions divorced from the actual experiences of Buddhists and Christians? There are also Buddhists who refuse to apply the word *mysticism* to the Buddhist Way. For example, Keiji Nishitani thought that while mysticism is common in Christianity and Islam, the closest thing to mysticism in Buddhism is the *myōkōnin* ("superior man"), who through the practice of *nenbutsu* ("Buddha reflection") experienced the presence of Amida Buddha. By way of further examples, Ueda Shizuteru, in comparing Meister Eckhart to Zen Buddhism, concluded that Zen is a nonmystical practice, while D. T. Suzuki declared that Zen had nothing to do with mysticism.[6]

Nevertheless, participants in current Buddhist–Christian interior dialogue seem to agree that there exists an affinity between Christian mystical tradition and what Buddhists look for through the practice of meditation. First, nearly all the questions and issues discussed by Christian mystical writers are also discussed in the Buddhist Way. Particularly in Zen, Awakening is described as a sudden and unexpected breakthrough of consciousness during, and sometimes after, the practice of meditation. Yet Buddhist meditation masters teach that there are no causal links between the efforts monks or nuns put into the practice of meditation and the actual attainment of the Awakening experience. The classical expression of this lack of a causal link is Dōgen's famous statement: "Practice and attainment are one."[7] In other words, meditative practice is not a means to Awakening and Awakening is not the result of the practice of meditation. This was particularly true for Dōgen.[8] Awakening just happens when and where it happens. All meditation does is prepare one for the possibility of an Awakening experience. But meditation does not guarantee the achievement of Awakening.

---

5. Merton, *Zen and the Birds of Appetite*, 57.
6. See Nishitani, *Religion and Nothingness*; Suzuki, "Satori," 201–16.
7. See Masunaga's translation of Dōgen's *Shōbōgenzō* in *A Primer of Sōtō Zen*, 38–39.
8. Kim, *Dōgen Kigen: Mystical Realist*, 296–308.

Christian mystical writers seem to be in agreement with Buddhists on this point. There are no causal links between the practice of contemplative disciplines like *lectio divina* ("divine reading"), centering prayer, and contemplative prayer and the achievement of either apophatic experiences of union with God or kataphatic experiences like visions, auditions, or awareness of God's presence. In Christian language, union with God or awareness of God's presence happens only because of God's grace. Nothing human beings do causes these experiences even as what human beings do might prepare for the possibility of their occurrence. And in point of fact, both Christian spiritual advisors and Buddhist meditation instructors insist that one should not practice contemplative prayer or meditation for any ulterior motives like experiencing God or becoming Awakened. In other words, to experience God either apophatically or kataphatically requires giving up the desire to experience God. Likewise in Buddhism, to achieve Awakening ultimately means renouncing the desire to achieve Awakening. Christian contemplative practices and Buddhist meditation are their own reward.

Some Evidence from the Cognitive Sciences[9]

Encouraged by thirty years of physical evidence of the human brain's plasticity, cognitive scientists are now taking a keen interest in the disciplines of meditation in Buddhism and the disciplines of Christian contemplative traditions. For example, Richard Davidson at the University of Wisconsin–Madison has been studying the brain activity of Tibetan Buddhist monks in both meditative and nonmeditative states. Davidson had earlier demonstrated that people inclined to fall prey to negative emotions display a pattern of persistent activity in the right prefrontal cortex. In those with more positive temperaments, the activity occurs in the left prefrontal cortex. When Davidson ran his experiment on a group of senior Tibetan monks skilled in meditation, the monks' baseline activity was much further to the left than anyone had previously demonstrated.[10]

In the wake of Davidson's work, a number of experiments monitoring brain waves using the electroencephalograms of individual Zen Buddhist monks and nuns during sessions of meditation have also been performed. Brain waves are a measure of the aggregate activities of large groups of

9. For a fuller discussion, see Ingram, *Buddhist-Christian Dialogue in an Age of Science*, 93–106.

10. Reported in Shreeve, "Beyond the Brain," 31.

neurons within specific areas of the brain and allow researchers to detect broad neurological patterns during specific kinds of activities. In one of the more widely known experiments on Zen monks, it was discovered that meditative states corresponding to distinctive brain-wave patterns, and that transitions into more advanced stages of meditation correlated with further brain-wave changes.[11]

It was found that each monk went through four distinct stages during each meditation session, beginning with alpha waves (typical of inward and focused attention and of deep relaxation) and ending, for more advanced monks, with theta waves, which are normally associated with drowsiness and hypnotic states. Only those who had meditated for more than twenty years showed theta activity. Also, the Zen master who guided the monks' practice could accurately distinguish between those monks who were at different meditative states without resorting to brain-wave data. Barring the existence of extra-sensory perception, the Zen master was quite able to discern the achievements of his students' practice because of his own years of training in meditation.

Of course, this experimental data neither proves nor disproves Buddhist doctrinal claims about wakening, *or* that Awakening is reducible to brain states. I know of no Buddhist teacher who argues that neuroscientific data proves the teachings of Buddhism. But brain-imaging research does suggest that that the disciplined practice of meditation over time can lead to kinds of experience that are, to some degree, quantifiable. In the case of Zen, prolonged meditation leads to a distinctive pattern of brain activity, and these patterns probably correlate with specific kinds of experiences, including the experience of Awakening if and when it occurs.

One possible implication of this empirical data is that mystical experiences produced by the practice of meditation are not merely the result of cultural conditioning, one of the "fallacies of misplaced concreteness" presupposed by Stephan Katz's analysis of mysticism.[12] If mystical experiences are merely the result of particular religious and cultural contexts, then the physiological states observed and measured during prolonged periods of meditation should not be observable cross-culturally. But it appears to be the case that cultural contexts over time produce new physiological states, which in turn evolve into new cultural possibilities. That is, levels of human experiences turn out to be biologically and environmentally interdepen-

11. See Peterson, *Minding God*, 106–7.
12. Katz, "Language, Epistemology, and Mysticism," 22–74.

dent—even for mystics. This may be one reason that most contemporary Buddhists do not normally experience the cognitive sciences as a threat but as empirical evidence that supports Buddhist doctrines, particularly the doctrines of impermanence, nonself, and dependent co-origination.[13]

Exploring how the cognitive sciences can function as a lens for theological reflection on a number of Christian doctrines is central to the work of Eugene d'Aquili and Andrew Newberg, who coined the term *neurotheology* to describe their work. According to their theoretical framework, the human mind functions through an interdependent filter of seven "cognitive operators," which are analogous to Immanuel Kant's categories, that act on external stimuli the brain continually receives from the external world. The seven cognitive operators are: (1) the holistic operator, (2) the reductionist operator, (3) the causal operator, (4) the abstractive operator, (5) the binary operator, (6) the quantative operator, and (7) the emotional operator.[14]

According to d'Aquili and Newburg, the causal operator is responsible for seeking out causal relationships, and the reductionist operator analyzes an object or idea in terms of its parts, By contrast, the holistic operator tries to integrate parts into a larger whole or gestalt. D'Aquili and Newberg locate these cognitive operators within specific areas of the brain, but the evidence for the locations of some cognitive operators (for example the emotional operator identified with the limbic system) is better than the evidence for the location of other operators (such as the binary operator, which is not assigned to any specific region in the brain).

The core element of d'Aquili and Newberg's work is their account of how "experiences of absolute unitary being" (AUB)—their term for apophatic experiences of union with no awareness of subject–object duality—arise in the brain. According to them, activities like ritual performance and meditation work toward achieving various levels of AUB by causing a cascade of physical reactions in the brain that stimulate emotional pathways at the same time that areas of the parietal lobe in the cerebral cortex associated with spatial orientation are cut off in a process called "differentiation." Given that the parietal lobe is involved with spatial awareness and self-other awareness, blocking off these areas would, they claim, result in the emergence of apophatic experience or, in their depiction, AUB. Differentiation is said to occur as the result of overstimulation of the sympathetic and parasympathetic systems in the brain, which are, according to d'Aquili

13. See Wallace, *Hidden Dimensions*, chaps. 4–6.
14. D'Aquili and Newberg, *The Mystical Mind*, 50–52.

and Newberg, responsible for states of arousal as well as quiescence. Normally, these two systems compete with each other. Religious activities like repetitive ritual dancing or chanting or focused meditation, however, often result in a kind of spillover effect that activates both systems. When this happen, the differentiation between these two systems disappears, and apophatic experiences of union (AUB) are activated.

D'Aquili and Newberg's work suggests that brain states are the primary causal agents in the formation of apophatic experiences (AUB). It is this conclusion that stimulates Buddhist dialogue with the cognitive sciences, since Awakening, an apophatic experience, is something pursued by an individual meditator's self-discipline and effort. But for Christian traditions of practice, the question of the causation of religious experiences is of greater theological importance because such experiences are understood to have God as their source. In other words, Buddhist nontheism seems to fit more tightly with d'Aquili and Newberg's research than does Christian monotheism. But d'Aquili and Newberg have given SPECT (Single Photon Emission Computed Tomography) scans to Franciscan nuns engaged in centering and contemplative prayer. Here too the SPECT scans showed differentiation in left parietal love, which, they claimed, confirmed that the nuns experienced apophatic experiences (AUB) during times of focused prayer.[15]

If, however, SPECT scans do in fact reveal the physical component of religious experiences like apophatic union or AUB, should the conclusion be that what shows up on the SPECT scans of Buddhist meditators or Franciscan nuns at prayer do not support Buddhism's worldview, or that God is the source of the Franciscan nun's experiences? Are such experiences merely self-generated by the concentration and verbalization that normally accompanies the practice of prayer? The scans of the nuns' brains did indicate heightened activity in the forebrain and verbal-association areas. But this is to be expected in any verbal undertaking. Moreover, since prayer is not always accompanied by apophatic experiences of union—a fact attested to by most Christians—at the moment it remains unclear how the EEG data gathered by d'Aquili and Newberg about Franciscan nuns at prayer should be interpreted.

But also at this stage of neurological research, what *is* clear is that continual practice of disciplines such as meditation, centering prayer, and contemplative prayer produce changes in the electrical activity of the brain so

15. Ibid., 147–54.

A THEOLOGICAL REFLECTION ON MYSTICAL EXPERIENCE

that both the conscious and unconscious activities of the mind are brought closer together. Conscious mental activity seems to impinge on unconscious mental activity, and vice versa, which opens the mind to awareness of God if one is a Christian, Jew, or Muslim, and to the experience of Awakening if one is a Buddhist. Both experiences are interpretations of what originates in the dark and subliminal depths of one's own being in a process analogous to, but different from, dreaming. The evidence supporting this tentative "conclusion in process" rests on neurological interpretation of the four brain-wave patterns measured by EEG:[16]

1. Beta is the most common pattern, and is what we experience during our waking hours. Beta consciousness measures thirteen or more cycles per second and is associated with focused attention and the active thinking of the mind focused on the external world. In Beta rhythm the highest degree of cortical stimulation is manifested.

2. Alpha waves produce more rest than beta waves. Wave frequency lowers to between eight to twelve cycles per minute, and the internal state of consciousness is described as a "relaxed awareness," with a movement toward interiority, or what neuroscientists call "internally focused states." Most people produce alpha waves when they close their eyes and relax. Continuing alpha consciousness with eyes open is difficult and can rarely be done without effort and seems to be one of the characteristics of adepts in Zen. High-amplitude alpha waves indicate a rather deep state of concentration. High-amplitude alpha waves are associated with more advanced stages of meditation and with apophatic mystical experiences.

3. The theta wave pattern exhibits four to seven cycles per second, is associated with drowsiness, and is the rhythm that appears when one slips into unconsciousness or sleep. Theta waves are often accompanied by dream-like imagery.

4. The delta wave pattern exhibits zero to four cycles per second and is the rhythm of deep sleep.

Brain-wave measurements indicate that people who meditate or practice centering or contemplative prayer enter rather easily into alpha. The converse is also probably true: alpha producers veer towards meditation and the contemplative life. But while all meditation or contemplation is alpha,

---

16. For a more detailed description of these wave patterns, see Johnston, *Silent Music*, 33–41.

not all alpha is contemplative. Meditation and contemplation are much more than a certain kind of brain wave because EEG research neglects the whole area of motivation, of faith, of grace and everything else that mystics experience which transcends scientific experimentation (including the doctrinal traditions guiding the disciplines of mystical practice).

While neurological research raises important questions about how we should think about religious experience in general and mystical experience in particular, the neurological foundations of all religious experience seem to create a bit of a paradox: as neurological research seems to confirm the reality of mystical experience, it simultaneously threatens to undermine the doctrinal claims of all religious Ways. So the most that can be affirmed at this point in time is that cognitive-scientific research on religious experience, particularly mystical experience, is still in its infancy.

SEVEN

The Jesus Way of Living without a Why

IN AN OBSERVATION SUPPORTED by contemporary process theology, Stephen of Hungary is reported somewhere to have said that without a past, human beings have no future.[1] I take this to mean that for the sake of our collective future possibilities, we must remember what the past has brought us. Whitehead called this "prehending" the past. We only know, even if incompletely, what we have experienced. And we need to remember what we know in order to anticipate what the future might or might not be. It sounds quite easy: remembering what we know. But there is no better definition of faith, and, of course, it is not possible to have faith other than through God's grace, as Lutherans like me think. Remembering and knowing are the *yin* and *yang*, the defining polarities of faith. True faith has little to do with belief in doctrines, even as doctrines may occasionally express faith.

Still, knowing and doubting are two interdependent sides of the same faith-coin, whose value lies in an exchange for knowledge that can crystallize options, buy nothing, or work together for profit as questions. For knowing and doubting are really saying, I don't know, but . . . and can lead us to ask, what then is certain? And if the question is pursued in fact, not fancy, it may bring us to new knowledge. But if we are unfaithful, we forget. We forget our own experiences, which have shown us that the unknown exists, and that we are contained in it as if by a cloud of unknowing. We know this when we can remember those times when we came up against the boundary limits of our knowing and the fact that there is something

---

1. Stephen I, also called Saint Stephen, in Hungarian Szent István. His original name is Vajk (born c. 970–975, and died August 15, 1038). He was canonized 1083. The first king of Hungary, he is considered to be the founder of the Hungarian state.

beyond our limits; mostly because we have occasionally experienced miracles: inner and outer events that cannot be explained by anything we know.

So I am certain that the unknown surrounds me—and everyone and everything else caught in the field of space–time. Mostly I forget this. But when I remember, I know the unknown—a "Cloud of Unknowing"—at least as much as it can be known.[2] And for a while, I become open to it, experience my relation to it, and apprehend that it is the source of all knowing. Then I understand that it is the unknown that remembers me, and that in remembering me I find my own particular meaning.

Of course, remembering the past and glimpsing the future possibilities to which the past points is never an individual achievement but rather a communal achievement over time, in which communities of individuals, in various ways and means, "participate" (to paraphrase Paul Tillich's understanding of symbols). Buddhists participate in a communal memory of a twenty-five-hundred-year-old historical narrative that remembers the life and teachings of Gautama the Buddha through a complex plurality of teachings and practices that have evolved over time. Jews remember a thirty-five-hundred-year-old covenant narrative recorded in the Tanakh, and rabbinic opinion recorded in the Talmud through an amazing plurality of Jewish ritual observances, legal decisions, and ethical teachings that have evolved over time. Muslims participate in a seventeen-hundred-year-old communal narrative centering on God's revelations to the Prophet Mohammed recorded in the Qur'an, and his applications of God's revelations recorded in the Sunna (Tradition). This narrative also takes into account later legal decisions that interpreted (and still interpret) the evolving meaning of revelation and tradition according to which Muslims test and measure their "surrender" (*islam*) to God. And Christians participate in a two-thousand-year communal memory preserved in the collective narratives of the Tanakh and the New testament, in the theological reflections of the church fathers and mothers, in Eastern Orthodox traditions of practice and theological reflection, in medieval Roman Catholic traditions of practice and theological reflection, in the Protestant Reformation, in neo-orthodox theology, in liberal theology (both Catholic and Protestant), and, yes, in process theology. These narratives have all evolved over time, and center on God's incarnation in the historical Jesus, affirmed to be the Christ of faith.

---

2. *The Cloud of Unknowing* is an anonymous fourteenth-century mystical text composed in Middle English. See Gallacher, *The Cloud of Unknowing*.

THE JESUS WAY OF LIVING WITHOUT A WHY

Mostly, as everyone who knows me can attest, I agree with Marcus Borg's judgment that the historical Jesus was a Galilean mystic who taught a subversive wisdom that can be characterized as (in the language of Marguerite Porete) "living without a why."[3] But I also think that Pieter F. Craffert's depiction of the historical Jesus as a Galilean mystical shaman is quite credible, since mystics cross-culturally undergo shamanic experiences like visions, auditions, travels to other dimensions, out-of-body experiences, and healings of disease and of demon possession.[4] Finally, I agree with Douglas A. Oakman's analysis of the historical Jesus as a socially engaged political radical who challenged the oppressive domination systems of his culture as a tax resister, an advocate of debt release, and a broker of divine healing and restoration of honor for the poor and marginal, who constituted perhaps 95 percent of the population of his society. Jesus's political activism was the direct cause of his arrest, trial, and execution by the authorities he challenged.[5] Of course, not all mystics are political radicals. But in point of fact, the history of religions is replete with mystics who also entered the rough-and-tumble of political struggle against oppressive domination systems: the eighth-, seventh-, and sixth-century prophets of Israel and Judah; Confucian and Daoist sages throughout Chinese history; Mohammed; Marguerite Porete; Martin Luther King Jr.; Mahatma Gandhi; and in contemporary Buddhism, Thich Nhat Hanh (to cite only a few).

Mystics are known in all of humanity's religious Ways. As I have noted in this book, mystical experiences cross-culturally involve vivid and sometimes frequent nonordinary states of conscious awareness, and take a number of different forms. Sometimes, there is a vivid sense of journeying into another dimension of reality, which is also the classic experience of shamans the world over.[6] Sometimes, there is a strong sensation of another reality coming upon one, as in "The Spirit fell upon me"—also a typical shamanic experience. Sometimes, an experience is of nature or a natural object momentarily transfigured by the Sacred shining through it: Moses saw a burning bush that was not consumed; John of the Cross apprehended

---

3. Borg, *Meeting Jesus Again for the First Time*, 30.

4. Craffert writes that "Borg's remarks that Jesus' baptism in the wilderness is strikingly similar to what is reported of charismatic persons cross-culturally," specifically shamans. His thesis is that this should be the starting point for understanding the life of Jesus as a "Galilean shamanic figure" (Craffert, *The Life of a Galilean Shaman*, 43, 214–59).

5. See Oakman, *The Political Aims of Jesus*, chap. 4.

6. See Eliade, *Shamanism*.

that the whole earth was filled with the "glory of God," where glory meant something like "radiant presence." In other words, in mystical or shamanic experience, the world is apprehended in such way that previous conventional perceptions seem like illusions.

All persons who have had such experiences share a strong sense that there is more to reality than the tangible world perceived in ordinary sensory experience. They seem to share a compelling sense of having experienced something real they did not know before. That is, their experiences are not merely emotive but noetic: not just a feeling of ecstasy, but one of knowing reality—the way things really are—by experience (like the way water tastes to a thirsty person crossing a hot dessert). Those who have had such experiences replace the conventional wisdoms of their religious traditions and cultures with the subversive wisdom of "living without a why." What such persons know by experience is what historians of religions like me generically name the Sacred.

Certainly, the specific religious Ways of humanity do not name the object of such experiences so abstractly. Rather they name it in particular ways: as Yahweh, Brahman, Atman, Allah, God, the Dao, or (in Lakota spirituality) Wankan Tanka (the Great Mysterious). The impulse to name the Sacred within specific religious, historical, and cultural contexts flows out of mystical experiences of a Sacred Reality that transcends all names, but that can apparently occur only within the limitations of specific historical and cultural contexts. The most common name for the Sacred in Jewish, Christian, and Islamic experience is God. Accordingly, I shall use the word *God* when referring to the experiences and teachings of the historical Jesus.

A second characteristic that most, but not all, mystics and shamans share is that because of their experiences they become mediators of the Sacred to their communities in a variety of specific ways. Sometimes they speak of the will of God or of how God works in the world. Sometimes they mediate the power of God through healings and exorcisms. Sometimes they function as game finders or rainmakers in hunter-gathering societies. What such persons have in common is that they become conduits by which the power of the Sacred enters into the world and the life of a community.

Examples of such persons whose communal memories are preserved in the biblical narratives abound. Abraham and Moses experienced visions of God and other paranormal experiences. In particular, the narratives about Moses's experiences of Yahweh placed him in the center of first Israelite and later Jewish faith and practice. He ascended Mount Sinai and while on the summit was in intimate communion with God. According to the book of Exodus, after he descended the mountain, his face glowed with God's presence. The point of these stories about Moses's encounter with God is very clear: he knew God "face to face," that is, "one-on-one," and lived to tell about it until the day he died, according to the end of the book of Deuteronomy (Deut 34:10). Thereby Moses was empowered to lead the Israelites out of slavery in Egypt into the freedom of a covenant agreement between the people of Israel and Yahweh.

The eighth-, seventh-, and sixth-century prophets of Israel and Judah were also mystics, and some underwent shamanic experiences. All had direct kataphatic and/or apophatic experiences of God's presence on the basis of which they, in harmony with the Mosaic traditions of covenant with God, felt called to challenge the unjust domination structures external to Israel—the empires of Assyria, Babylon, and Persia—and the unjust internal domination systems of Israelite society. John Dominic Crossan points to two Judean mystics closer to the time of the historical Jesus: Honi the Circle-Drawer and Hanina ben Dosa.[7] Both of these men were famous for their contemplative prayer and their abilities as "miracle-workers."[8] Finally, a Pharisaic Israelite named Saul of Tarsus, according to the book of Acts, had a mystical vision of the risen Jesus as the Christ on the Damascus Road, which involved an experience of blinding light and a voice that transformed Saul from a persecutor of the early Jesus movement into an apostle named Paul (Acts 9:3–9). Paul also described an experience of a journey into the "third heaven" and an experience of things that cannot be put into words because they transcended the categories of language (2 Cor 12:1–4).

In short, Israelite tradition in Jesus's day preserved powerful communal memories of persons who had kataphatic and apophatic experiences of God. It seems to me that according to the earliest historical accounts in the Synoptic Gospels, Jesus was most certainly a Galilean shamanic mystic whose experiences motivated everything he did and said, particularly his

---

7. Crossan, *The Historical Jesus*, 142–56, ; see also Borg, *Meeting Jesus Again for the First Time*, 34–35.

8. During a time of severe drought, Honi drew a circle in the dust, stood inside it, and informed God that he would not move until it rained. When it began to drizzle, Honi told God that he was not satisfied and expected more rain, at which point it began to pour. Honi then informed God that he wanted a calm rain, at which point the rain calmed. Hanina was a student of Rabbi Johanan ben Zakkai. When the rabbi's son became ill, he asked Hanina to pray for his son. The son recovered and the overjoyed father could not refrain from expressing his admiration for Hanina, stating that he himself might have prayed the whole day without doing any good.

political activism. He experienced kataphatic visions, including a vision during his baptism, in which, as the prophet Ezekiel is recorded to have experienced, Jesus saw "the heavens open" and the Spirit descending on him like a dove (Mark 1:10). Particularly important was Jesus's journey alone into the desert narrated as the temptation stories, but which historians of religions and anthropologists recognize as a wilderness ordeal or vision quest. Jesus also employed practices like fasting, and engaged in long periods of what is now called contemplative prayer or wordless meditation. In all probability, it was during his sojourn in the desert that Jesus experienced apophatic union with God. Exactly how Jesus practiced these contemplative disciplines is not known. But they were probably similar to the contemplative disciplines preserved in Judaism, Christianity, and Islamic practice traditions.

Other evidence that Jesus was a Galilean mystic derives from how he addressed God. His language was very intimate, particularly in his use of *Abba*, which is an Aramaic word that a small child might have used to address the biological father. *Abba* is much like the English word *father*. (It must also be noted that Jesus also referred to God with female images.) What seems likely is that Jesus's way of speaking about God expressed the intimacy of his own mystical awareness of God's presence everywhere at all times and in all places. Jesus was not simply a person who *believed* in the existence of God; he *knew* the existence of God *by experience*.

Consequently, evidence within the Synoptic Gospels and in the general history of religions points to Jesus as a particular type of religious person known cross-culturally. This evidence seems to undercut a pervasive notion in conservative and fundamentalist forms of Christian tradition that portray the historical Jesus as unique. The notion of Jesus's uniqueness is also linked to the ideas that Christianity is exclusively the only true religion and that Jesus is the "only way." Jesus was not God, and did not claim to be either God or the Messiah. Rather than being the exclusive revelation of God, he was one of many mystical mediators of the Sacred. This conclusion does not subtract from the theological importance of Jesus for Christian faith and practice, but in fact adds to the credibility of both Jesus *and* Christian faith. For at the center of Jesus's life was a profound and continuous experience of God in, with, and under all things and events. What separated Jesus from his contemporaries was that the life he lived and the death he died was wrapped up in his continual experience of God's presence.

THE JESUS WAY OF LIVING WITHOUT A WHY

Furthermore, like most mystics, Jesus was a teacher of wisdom—a "sage," as wisdom teachers are commonly called. This is perhaps the strongest consensus among contemporary Jesus scholars. There are two types of wisdom, which means that there are two types of sages. The most common wisdom is conventional wisdom, and its teachers are conventional sages. Conventional wisdom is what everybody knows, a culture's understanding about what is real and how to live. The second type of wisdom is an alternative, subversive wisdom that undermines conventional wisdom and points to another path or way of life. Its teachers are subversive sages. For example, the historical Buddha and the Daoist sage Zhuangzi taught a way that leads away from conventional perceptions and values toward a way of life that reflects "the way things really are." The wisdom of subversive sages is the wisdom of "the road less traveled," whose basic character is "living without a why." The same is true for the historical Jesus. His wisdom spoke of "the narrow way" that leads to life and that subverts "the broad way" followed by conventional human beings, which leads to death. But to understand the "narrow Way" of which Jesus spoke, it is necessary to consider what Jesus taught about "living without a why."

It is well established that Jesus, like the Buddha and Confucius, was an oral teacher who employed aphorisms and parables. Aphorisms are short, easy-to-remember sayings, like great one-liners. Parables are essentially short stories. Together, the aphorisms and parables preserved in the Synoptic Gospels place us directly in contact with the voice of the historical Jesus. According to contemporary Jesus scholarship, the most certain thing we know about him, since he lived in a culture where literacy rates were quire low, was that he was a storyteller and speaker of great one-liners. The aphorisms and parables of Jesus are invitational forms of speech. Jesus used them to invite his hearers to apprehend something they might not have otherwise apprehended. In this invitation they tease imagination into action, suggest more than they directly say, and invite a transformation of perception and understanding. In many ways, they function like koans in Zen Buddhist meditational practices.

Jesus's use of aphorisms, of which there are more than a hundred recorded in the three Synoptic Gospels (Matthew, Mark, and Luke), are crystallizations of insight that invite further reflection and that, more often than not, generate startling insights:

"You cannot serve two masters."
"You cannot get grapes from a bramble bush."

"If a blind person leads a blind person, will they not both fall into a ditch?"

"Leave the dead to bury the dead."

"You strain out a gnat and swallow a camel."

These are all short provocative one-liners that say more than their literal meanings and invite hearers to apprehend something they otherwise might not understand.[9]

Jesus's aphorisms were probably spoken one at a time, but this is not how they appear in the Synoptic Gospels, where they are typically grouped into collections of sayings. Aphorisms are also said many times. No oral teacher, especially an itinerant teacher like Jesus, uses a one-liner only once. This means that their particular context described in the gospel narratives was not the sole context in which they were heard. It is perhaps best to imagine Jesus's aphorisms as repeated pieces of oral teaching employed many times on different occasions.

Some of the parables are very short, as brief as a typical aphorism, with the only difference between aphorism and parable being that parables are narratives. Jesus's short parables, like aphorisms, are memorable, enigmatic sayings complete in themselves. For example:

> "To what should I compare the kingdom of God? It is like yeast that a woman took and mixed three measures of flower until all of it was leavened." (Luke 13:20 = Matt 13:33)

> "The kingdom of heaven is like treasure hidden in a field, which someone found and hid; then in his joy he goes and sells all that he has and buys that field." (Matt 13:44).

But most of Jesus's recorded parables are similar to short stories with plot and character development. It is probable that Jesus would have told them numerous times in different ways and may have expanded them to different lengths depending on his audience.

Jesus employed aphorisms and parables to subvert conventional wisdom and replace it with subversive wisdom. Conventional wisdom is the dominant wisdom of any culture, a culture's most taken-for-granted understandings about the way things are, and about the way to live in harmony with the way things are. Conventional wisdom, in other words, summarizes a culture's dominant worldview. Conventional wisdom is a culture's social

---

9. Luke 16:13 = Matt 6:24; Luke 6:44 = Matt 7:16; Luke 6:39 = Matt 5:14; Luke 9:60 = Matt 8:22; Matt 23:24. See, e.g., Hedrick, *The Wisdom of Jesus*.

construction of reality and the internalization of that construction within the psyche of individuals. Therefore, it offers guidance about how to live, and covers everything from highly practical issues such as etiquette to images of the good life. Moreover, conventional wisdom is supported by a system of rewards and punishments. You reap what you sow; follow this way and all will go well; you receive what you deserve; the righteous will prosper. These are the constant messages of conventional wisdom. Finally, conventional wisdom has both social and psychological consequences. Socially, conventional wisdom creates a world of hierarchies and boundaries. Some of these are inherited, and are exemplified when differences in gender, race, or physical condition are given hierarchical values and roles. Psychologically, conventional wisdom becomes the basis for personal identity and self-esteem. Politically, conventional wisdom is the ideological foundation of oppressive social, political, and economic systems of injustice.

Like all mystical teachers of subversive wisdom, Jesus used the language of reversal to utterly shatter the conventional wisdom of his time. For example, what kind of world is it when a Samaritan—a outsider and a ritually impure person—can be good, indeed the hero of a story told to Judeans? What kind of world is it when a Pharisee—conventionally viewed as righteous and pure—can be pronounced unrighteous while an outsider can be accepted? What kind of world is it when riding bareback on a jackass can be a symbol of kingship? What kind of world is it when purity is a matter of the heart and not a matter of external boundaries? In what kind of world are the poor honored?[10] What kind of world is it when the first are last, and the last first? In what kind of world are the humble exalted and the exalted humbled? The world Jesus taught was the kingdom of God. Jesus compared God's kingdom to something small, like a mustard seed. Jesus likened the kingdom of God to something impure, like a woman (associated with impurity), and like putting leaven (which is impure) into flour. Jesus noted that the kingdom is for children, who in his world were nobodies, which means the kingdom of God is a kingdom of nobodies.[11] The kingdom is also for outcasts (for tax collectors, prostitutes, the poor, the sick, and the lame), not for those whom conventional wisdom lifts up as worthy of God's favor.

---

10. See K. C. Hanson, "How Honorable! How Shameful!: A Cultural Analysis of Matthew's Makarisms and Reproaches."

11. See Crossan, *Jesus*, chap. 3.

So like most sages, Jesus spoke of two ways of life: a conventional way and a foolish way, a way of life and a way of death, a narrow way and a broad way. For example,

> Enter through the narrow gate; for the gate is wide and the way is easy that leads to destruction, and there are many who take it. For the gate is narrow and the way is hard that leads to life, and there are few who find it. (Matt 7:13–14)

For most persons everywhere at all time and in all places, the wise way is the way of conventional wisdom, and the foolish way is the path of disregard for conventional wisdom. Jesus reversed this understanding: he spoke of and taught that the broad way, the way of conventional wisdom, is the way of foolishness and leads to personal and communal destruction. So he attacked the central values of his social world's culture: family, wealth, honor, purity, and conventional religion. It was against these values that he directed some of his most radical aphorisms and parables.

For example, in Jesus's culture the family, which was a patriarchal structure, was the primary social unit and the center of both identity and economic security. So a good family experiences God's blessings. But Jesus spoke of leaving family and "hating" family: "Whoever comes to me and does not hate father and mother, wife and children, brothers and sisters, yes, and even life itself, cannot be my disciple" (Luke 14:26). These words are probably directed against the patriarchal family structure, the primary social unit of Jesus's culture that was also a microcosm of the wider hierarchal social system in which he lived. The thing to note in this aphorism is that it is one among many instances of Jesus's using the image of God as Father in a way that subverted the patriarchy of his culture.

Furthermore, far from seeing wealth as a blessing from God for having lived wisely, Jesus understood the preoccupation with wealth as idolatry: "you cannot serve God and wealth" (Matt 6:25/Luke19:13). He told numerous stories of people whose preoccupation with possessions caused them to miss the banquet to which everyone is invited. For instance, one parable features a farmer who spends his life gathering his goods into barns and then dies before he really begins to live. Another parable includes a rich man who day after day ignores the beggar at his gate (Luke 14:16–24 = Matt 21:1–10). Jesus also ridiculed those concerned with honor, castigated those concerned with rules of purity, and harshly indicted those who trusted in their own religiosity. It is easy to see that those who trusted the conventional wisdom of Jesus's culture found much in his sayings and parables offensive and threatening, as do conventional persons living today.

Jesus's rejection of conventional wisdom is particularly evident in the way he experienced God. Jesus invited his hearers to apprehend God neither as a judge, nor as a deity whose requirements must be met, but as gracious and compassionate. This is clear in two of the most familiar sayings of Jesus:

> "Look at the birds of the air; they neither sow nor reap nor gather into barns, and yet your heavenly Father feeds them."

> "Consider the lilies of the field, how they grow; they neither toil nor spin, yet I tell you, even Solomon in all his glory was not clothed like one of these." (Matt 6:26–29= Luke 12:24–27)

In other words, Jesus characterized reality—"the way things really are"—as overflowing with cosmic generosity and life. Yet there is also a deep realism in these sayings because in the very next line, Jesus speaks of the lilies of the field today being beautiful and tomorrow being thrown into ovens: "But if God so clothes the grass of the field, which is alive today and tomorrow is thrown into the oven, will he not much more clothe you—you of little faith?" (Matt 6:30/Luke 12:28). At the foundations of Jesus's invitation to see God as the source of life as gracious and generous, there is a deep reality therapy at work that recognizes the impermanence of life.

But for me, the parable that best summarizes Jesus's image of God as compassionate is the parable of the Prodigal Son. Marcus Borg breaks this parable into three acts.[12] In act one, the prodigal son's life is described in detail: a life of going into exile and becoming an outcast. He journeys to a far country, that is, a Gentile country and therefore an impure land, and there he not only squanders his money in "loose living" but, reduced to poverty, ends up as a field hand working for a Gentile pig farmer. As a field hand working with pigs, he has become worse than untouchable, according to Israelite purification laws. Act 1 concludes with the Prodigal's coming to his senses and with his decision to return home.

In act 2 the focus is the father. Seeing his son at a distance, he "has compassion" and rushes to meet him. Before the prodigal son can speak, the father hugs and kisses him. Brushing aside his son's prepared confession, the father in great joy clothes his son with his best robe, and puts a

---

12. See Borg, *Meeting Jesus Again for the First Time*, 83–85.

ring on his finger and shoes on his feet: symbolic actions of acceptance and restoration. Then he orders the preparation of a banquet in his son's honor.

Meanwhile, act 3 begins with the sounds of music and dancing floating over a distant field where the father's elder son is working. When the elder son finds out what's going on, he refuses to join the banquet and celebration and complains that he has been dutiful and obedient and was never so treated by his father. The father begs him to join the celebration, and the parable ends with a unanswered question: will the elder son's conventional sense of the way things ought to be keep him away from the banquet?[13]

This parable, like others, represents a systematic subversion of the conventional wisdom of Jesus's time as well as of our time. Of course, the elder son's voice is the voice of most human beings. But the real point, it seems to me, is that the story of the prodigal son portrays a religious Way quite differently from the way of conventional wisdom: a life of exile in a "far country" and a journey of return, but never to a life of duty, requirements, and rewards. The historical Jesus, in other words, stood squarely within the Hebraic prophetic tradition. But living by subversive wisdom can be dangerous. Or to paraphrase the way Dietrich Bonhoeffer put it, "When God calls you, God calls you to your death."[14] Sometimes God calls us to a physical death, but most always God calls us to die to the conventional ways of living, according to which most persons (past and present) structure their lives. Religious faith always places persons at odds with conventional culture and the domination systems of culture because faithful persons find themselves unable to structure their lives according to the conventional worldview of the majority of human beings. Walking "the way less traveled" can get a person killed, as the historical Jesus experienced hanging on a cross, and as Marguerite Porete experienced burning in a fire in 1310.

But exactly what *is* the narrow way, the way less traveled that is the subversive wisdom of the historical Jesus? According to Marcus Borg, the evidence seems to indicate that Jesus invited his hearers to apprehend God

---

13. Luke 15:11–32. Borg, *Meeting Jesus Again for the First Time*, 85–88, notes that although this parable is found only in Luke, he thinks the consensus of New Testament scholarship is that it reflects the voice of Jesus, and Luke provides readers with a probably condensed oral story going back to Jesus. In a note I received from Oakman, he concluded that this parable reflects Jesus's own experiences as a prodigal (i.e., his own experience of radical grace), and the "elder brother" is his brother James.

14. Bonhoeffer's exact words are, "When Christ calls a man, he calls him to come and die." See Bonhoeffer, *The Cost of Discipleship*, 87.

as gracious and womblike rather than as an enforcer of requirements and boundaries. Second, Jesus's subversive wisdom was an invitation to a way of life that leads away from conventional wisdom to a life centered in God. The subversive wisdom of Jesus understands religious life as a deepening relationship with God, not as a life of requirements and rewards. Finally, Jesus's subversive wisdom teachings require resistance against exploitative social political, and economic systems that oppress the majority of human beings in any culture in every period of human history. That is to say, compassion and justice were for the historical Jesus the ying and yang of God's call to all human beings.[15]

This aspect of Jesus's Way often leads to the question of the role of judgment in his teachings. While there are numerous passages in the Synoptic Gospels that refer to a last judgment with eternal consequences, it seems to me that the notion that life is primarily about meeting God's requirements so that human beings might achieve a blessed afterlife was foreign to Jesus. In all probability, he believed in an afterlife, but his teachings had little, if anything, to do with how to get there. While some gospel passages portray Jesus speaking about a Last Judgment, I am convinced that the threat of being judged by God for one's sins was not central to his teachings, if such a threat was even present at all. However, the notion of historical judgment was most certainly part of his teachings about the narrow way in much the same way it was for the prophets that preceded Jesus: blindness has its consequences for both society and individuals. In both cases, living in the world of conventional wisdom is living in "the land of the dead." Today, all one need do is read a newspaper or watch the nightly news on television to confirm the reality of historical judgment. We in fact judge ourselves; this, not the threat of eternal punishment in a hellish afterlife, is that to which judgment points. Furthermore, given the structure of existence inherent in Jesus's Way, it is not likely that he referred to himself as Messiah or as God coming in the future to initiate the kingdom of God.

Jesus's narrow way is portrayed by another image; he spoke of the narrow way as a way of death: "Whoever does not carry the cross and follow me, cannot be my disciple."[16] Death as an image of the narrow way points to dying to the world of conventional wisdom as the center of one's security,

---

15. See See Oakman, *The Political Aims of Jesus*, chap. 5. See also Oakman, *Jesus and the Peasants*; Hanson and Oakman, *Palestine in the Time of Jesus*; and Oakman, *Jesus, Debt, and the Lord's Prayer*.

16. Luke 14:27 = Matt 10:38; Mark 8:34.

and points to dying to permanent selfhood. In other words, Jesus points to not clinging to permanent selfhood as the center of one's concern. Death is the ultimate letting go, and therefore the opposite of the clinging or grasping that is the defining characteristic of the life of conventional wisdom. The path of death, for Jesus, is simultaneously the path to new life. That is, it results in rebirth, a resurrection to a life centered in God. Or restated in the language of process theology, the creative transformation of perception that the historical Jesus knew through his own mystical experiences is one to which he invited his hearers.

The Jesus Way is, in other words, a life of compassionate struggle for justice. The Hebrew word Jesus used for *compassion* ("steadfast loving-kindness") is *ḥesed*, which has nothing to do with pity often associated by tough-minded English speakers with uncritical, unrealistic, sloppy, and indiscriminate benevolence to all. Compassion is not feeling sorry for people. The English word *compassion* comes from the Greek verb *pathein*, meaning "to endure something with another person." *Pathein* is very close in meaning to the Hebrew *ḥesed*: feeling another person's pain as if it were one's own, or another person's joy as if it were one's own, and acting toward that person accordingly. For in an independent universe created by God, another person's pain or joy *is* one's own pain or joy. In the Israelite prophetic tradition, compassion is summed up by the Golden Rule: positively, "Do to others what you would have them do to you"; and negatively, "Do not do to others what you would not like done to you."

So practicing compassion means looking within our own self-awareness, discovering what gives us pain, and refusing under any circumstances to inflict that pain on anybody or on any creature. This means that compassion for Jesus was the flipside of justice (*mishpat*), where justice means the "right treatment of people," giving people or groups of people what they need for meaningful existence. This may not always be what they want or what the domination systems that oppress the majority of human beings want. Compassion, for Jesus, was not merely a matter of feeling sympathy towards someone else, although it can and should include this. But emotions are ephemeral, meaning that they come and go. The compassionate justice that Jesus lived and taught as the heart of subversive wisdom demands an act of will and intellect, a conscious determination to dethrone oneself from the center of our conventionally constructed worlds as we put others in the center.

For these reasons the Way of Jesus is a serious challenge to conventional expressions of Christian tradition. This is so because following the Way of Jesus entails moving from conventional forms of institutionalized Christian tradition to the subversive wisdom of Jesus's Way. Conventional Christianity is a way of being religious based on believing what one has heard from others. It consists of asserting that life is about believing stuff about what the Bible says, or what the institutional church doctrinally teaches about what Christians are required to believe in order to be faithful. Conventional Christianity reduces faith to belief. The Way of Jesus, however, is a relationship to which the Bible and the theological traditions of the plurality of Christian traditions point: that reality that Jesus experienced as God and the Spirit of God.

Accordingly, Jesus's gospel is the good news of his own message—that there exists a way of living that moves beyond both secular and religious conventional wisdom. The creative transformation of which Jesus spoke leads from a life of requirements to a life of relationship with God and with everything that lives. The Way of Jesus replaces a life of anxiety with a life of peace and trust. It leads from the bondage of self-preoccupation to the freedom of self-forgetfulness. It leads from a conventional life centered in cultural standards to a subversive Way centered in God. It is, in other words, a Way engendered by God's grace, as Saint Paul, Saint Augustine, the mystics of Christian tradition, Martin Luther, and John Wesley, among others, knew and taught.

The Christ of Faith

It is the Way of Jesus that has convinced me that the historical Jesus is also the Christ of faith. By this I do not mean, the historical Jesus is God. I agree with the majority of mainline New Testament scholars that Jesus did not think of himself as divine or even as the Messiah (in Greek, *Christos*), as someone appointed by God to free Israel from oppressors and to establish a future peaceful world order with Jerusalem at the center. The early Jesus movement was a minority subgroup within first-century Judean religion. This means that the earliest witnesses to the historical Jesus—and to his resurrection—were participants in Judean religion, including Saint Paul during his mystical experience of the risen Christ on the Damascus Road. They lived as a minority within the wider community of Judean religion. They believed that the historical Jesus was resurrected from his grave. Some of the disciples are reported to have experienced the resurrected Jesus (Matthew 28; on the Road to Emmaus, in Luke 24:13–35, 36–49). Paul's and the disciples' experiences of Jesus's presence after his death were most probably kataphatic mystical experiences: visions, auditions, particular followers sensing Jesus's presence. It was these experiences that convinced the disciples that the historical Jesus was the Christ, the messiah who would usher in the kingdom or commonwealth of God, either in the near future or, as the later New Testament writers concluded, at an undisclosed time of God's choosing.

Of course, transforming the historical Jesus into the post-Easter Jesus declared to be the Messiah entailed for first-century Judeans a change in the meaning of the term *messiah*. Furthermore, for two thousand years Christians have been debating and promoting creeds about what the relation of the historical Jesus is to the Christ of faith. In other words, Christian faith hangs on the notion that the pre-Easter Jesus and the resurrected, post-Easter Jesus were the Incarnation of God. Without the experiences of the resurrection of the historical Jesus, the Christian Way would have probably reverted into Judean religion or perhaps simply vanished with the death of the first-generation disciples.

As was the case in the early Jesus communities, so today no universally accepted understanding of either Jesus's resurrection or of the Incarnation exists within the pluralism of contemporary Christian communities. Certainly, most Christians assert *that* the resurrection actually occurred, and that Jesus is God's incarnation in history. But exactly what all this means remains a hot topic of discussion particularly among Christian theologians. (I suspect the vast majority of Christians sitting in pews and most of their pastors are not particularly involved in this discussion, and do not care to be, even as they believe in the resurrection and the Incarnation.)

As I stated in chapter 3, the categories of process theology capture the early Jesus community's experience of the historical Jesus as the Christ, God's incarnation in a human life and in history. To genuinely hear the historical Jesus's subversive wisdom that radically, yet gently, points to his experience of God as compassionate and just means to experience Jesus as the Christ as an embodiment of the process of creative transformation at work everywhere in the universe. Experiencing such subversive wisdom creates cognitive dissonance in relation to every existing theological, economic, social, and political system. It is when what the conventional world takes for granted is rendered suspicious that one is open to the process of creative

THE JESUS WAY OF LIVING WITHOUT A WHY

transformation modeled by the historical Jesus. Or as Reinhold Niebuhr once noted, Jesus afflicted the comfortable and comforted the afflicted.

Of course creative transformation happens elsewhere in humanity's religious Ways. Sages—those mystics who experienced the Sacred however named—transmitted subversive wisdom contextualized by the cultures and religious Ways in which they lived and died. Sages like the Buddha, Sankara, the Daoist mystics, Mohammed, the Sufi mystics, Jewish mystics, and other nameless sages too numerous to count everywhere at all times and in all places incarnated and mediated the process of creative transformation to their communities. They still do. So to think of the historical Jesus as the Incarnation of God does not require asserting that he was the first and only incarnation of the process of creative transformation that Christians think originates in God as Jesus experienced God.

But from the point of view of Christian faith and practice (which *does not* invalidate or replace other religious Ways), the historical Jesus is the Christ of faith and practice. The question is, how was God related to Jesus so that he became the Christ of faith? Was Jesus only a Galilean shamanic mystic and teacher of subversive wisdom, or something else that emerged from Jesus's mystical experience as expressed in his subversive wisdom? Certainly, all attempts to describe the structure of existence of an individual are speculative inferences, particularly when that individual lived two thousand years ago.

For me, two characteristics of the sayings of Jesus preserved in his aphorisms and parables are central. First, his aphorisms and parables express an immediate and undistorted perception of the conditions of human existence—two thousand years ago and in the present. Second, Jesus spoke and acted with a peculiar authority, which went far beyond that of the prophets of Israel and Judah, even as what he said and did was thoroughly grounded in the prophetic traditions of the Judaism of his day. In other words, Jesus's structure of existence seems to have been distinctive in its mode of relating to God.

Classical Christology asserts God's presence in the historical Jesus, but in a way that unintentionally denies his full humanity. This reflects the substance metaphysics that underlies Greek philosophy through which early Christian memories of Jesus were translated into the intellectual traditions of the Hellenistic world. Certainly this process helped transform the original Jesus movement into a separate Way called Christianity, particularly as first- and second-century theologians entered into heated debates about the relation of God to the historical Jesus. Simply stated, Greek philosophy, undergirded by substance metaphysics, required that if the *logos* is present in Jesus, then some part of his human nature must have been displaced. So, as the Nicene Creed affirms, the defining substance or "stuff" that makes God God, and the defining "stuff" that makes Jesus human, existed in Jesus without "confusion." Hence, Jesus is both divine and human simultaneously, which is why he is declared to be "the Christ, the Son of the living God."

But the problem is, according to Greek substance metaphysics, every substance is different from every other substance. For example, according to Aristotle, all things and events are "formed substances." So the substance *formed* into a particular human being and the substances *formed* into a dog or cat or tree are not identical. So the question is, how can the substance that forms God (which makes God God) exist in a human being named Jesus, formed by a human substance "without confusion"? As far as I can tell, this puzzle has no coherent resolution if one sticks to the substance categories of classical Geek philosophy as a means of characterizing how Jesus's relation to God seems so distinctive for Christian faith and practice.

It seems to me that process theology has a more coherent way of characterizing Jesus's relation to God. It does so by abandoning the substance metaphysics of Greek philosophy and replacing it with the process category called "structure of existence." One way in which different structures of existence can be distinguished is by focusing on the constitution of the integrating center of experience, that is, the self or the *I*. When we are infants, this organizing center is controlled largely by our bodily experiences. However, normal adult experiences are constituted by the memory of our past experiences. Adult experiences are largely organized in terms of purposes and memories inherited from the past. It is this historical route of experiences that constitutes our self-identity through time.

Yet in all experiences the divine presence is also incarnated in the form of God's initial aim for all things and events: what process thinkers, following Whitehead, refer to as "actual occasions of experience." The initial aim from God is what is best for that occasion of experience at every moment of its existence in interdependence with every other occasion of experience in the universe. There is, however, tension between God's initial aim for an occasion and an occasion's subjective aim for itself. Accordingly, for the vast majority of human beings, the divine presence is experienced as other, occasionally as gracious, often as judgmental, or simply as absent.

THE JESUS WAY OF LIVING WITHOUT A WHY

The evidence from Jesus's aphorisms and parables suggests that his structure of existence did not reflect this tension because Jesus's selfhood seems to have been constituted by God's agency as initial aim in union with Jesus's own subjective aim for himself. According to Whitehead, God's initial aim for all occasions of experience is that each occasion achieves the maximum self-fulfillment of which it is capable in interrelationship with the totality of occasions that constitute the universe at any given moment of time; here *self-fulfillment* is defined as an intensity of beauty and harmony greater than the sum of its parts.[17]

From this perspective, God's initial aim for Jesus, and Jesus's subjective aim for himself, were, in Buddhist language, "nondual." Or as David Ray Griffin writes, "We may think of Jesus' structure of existence in terms of an 'I' that is co-constituted as much by divine agency within him as by his own personal past."[18] This means that the normal tensions between God's initial aim and the purposes received from the past—which express our subjective aim to achieve our own individual fulfillment—did not exist in the historical Jesus. Jesus's subjective aim for himself was conformed to God's initial aim for Jesus. This, in turn, created openness to God's call in each moment of Jesus's life. Whereas the Word or *logos* is incarnated in all things and events—in every human being—Christians can reasonably declare that the historical Jesus is the Christ because God's incarnation in the form of God's initial aim for Jesus constituted his very selfhood.

Consequently, the historical Jesus was fully human. But for whatever reason, he conformed his subjective aim for himself to God's initial aim for him: not my will, but "your will be done," as the Lord's Prayer has it (see Matt 6:5–14).[19] One can therefore reasonably affirm that while the Word, in the form of God's initial aim, is incarnated in all things and events at every moment of space–time, the historical Jesus became the Christ by identifying his subjective aim for himself with God's initial aim for Jesus. Or to cite words he is reported to have said to God on the night before he was killed,

---

17. Whitehead, *Process and Reality*, 108, 224, 244.
18. Cobb and Griffin, *Process Theology*, 105.
19. Jesus's conscious incorporation of God's initial aim into his own subjective aim for himself is the foundation of his teaching about surrendering to God's will. This memory of Jesus's experience and teaching is also preserved in the Qur'an, in which Jesus is portrayed as a prophet who practiced *Islam*, or "surrender to the will of God." Muslims continue to revere Jesus as a Muslim, meaning "one who surrendered to God's will." In fact, after Mohammed, more verses in the Qur'an are devoted to Jesus than to any other prophet mentioned in the Qur'an.

"Not my will, but your will" (see Mark 14:32–42). In my view, Jesus was no different than any other human being because, in the language of the Nicene Creed, "he was made man." But in the unity of his subjective aim with God's initial aim—God's will—he was in nondual harmony with the Christ (or in language from the Gospel of John) with the *logos* incarnated in all things and events (John 1:1–18).

EIGHT

Living without a Why: The Way of Grace

MAINLINE PROTESTANTS SINCE MARTIN Luther's break from the Roman Catholic Church five hundred years ago have been quite nervous about apophatic and kataphatic mystical experiences. This skepticism is rooted in Luther's writings. Yet as Steven Ozment notes, from 1516 to 1518 Luther had the highest regard for the German mystical tradition. In a letter to his friend Georg Apalatin, he described Johnanes Tauler's sermons as "pure and solid theology." In the same letter he professed to know of no contemporary work either in Latin or German more beneficial or in closer agreement with the Gospels. And when Luther defended the Ninety-Five Theses in 1518, he confessed that he could find no theology better than Tauler's mystical theology, which he judged to be superior to all the Scholastic theologians combined. In the same year he published his translation of an anonymous mystical text titled *German Theology*, declaring that only the Bible and Saint Augustine taught him more about "God, Christ, humanity, and all things."[1]

Yet Luther was also highly critical of mystical theology. The Scholastic theology undergirding the mysticism in his day elicited his constant criticism because of its emphasis on the "works" human beings must perform to achieve God's redemption: living ethically, participating in the Church's sacraments, believing and following the orthodox teachings of the Church, withdrawing from the world, practicing *lectio divina* and contemplative prayer. Furthermore, Luther was harshly critical of what he judged to be mystical theology's over-reliance on Aristotelian philosophy and good works. All these practices and traits of the medieval Church Marguerite Porete had previously criticized with the label "Holy Church the Little." For

---

1. See Ozment, *The Age of Reform*, 239–44.

Luther, the key religious problem became one of faith as trust, a transformation from a state of doubt and uncertainty to utter confidence in Christ as the Word of God incarnated in Scripture and in the historical Jesus. For Luther, this confidence in God only occurs as a gift of God's grace. Luther's specific question was, could God be depended upon to save those who could not fulfill God's law and who thereby remained unworthy? The question of personal salvation remained central to Luther's Augustinian assessment of God and human nature as totally under the domination of original sin.

Luther also had more practical reasons for his mistrust of mysticism, some of which I must admit that I share. For example, during Luther's lifetime, a number of movements commonly known as the left wing of the Reformation arose. He referred to these movements as *Schwëmer*, meaning "enthusiasts," a term he used to describe people with wild and overly emotional ideas. The enthusiasts were the fundamentalists of the Protestant Reformation. What many of the enthusiasts had in common was reliance on subjective religious experience as the defining character of Christian faith. One had to have such experiences—visions, auditions, experiences of speaking in tongues—to be Christian.

Luther rejected the enthusiasts because of their claim to discern the saving work of God outside Word and Sacrament, and also because of their overeager support of revolutionary political movements. He rejected all efforts to establish faith on subjective inner experience. In opposition to the enthusiasts, he used the Latin phrase *extra nos*, meaning "outside ourselves." In other words, we encounter God's grace as an external reality outside ourselves in Scripture, the preaching of the gospel, and in the sacraments, not merely or even primarily in the subjective depths of our experiences. But while I agree with Luther's conclusions in this regard, there is little evidence that the majority of Christian mystical writers used their experiences to support the doctrinal fundamentalisms of the enthusiast of their times. For them, this would have represented a regression into what Marguerite Porete called "Holy Church the Little."

Still, for Luther, the "means of grace" are hard, material facts. Scripture is a book all persons can read; the preacher stands in a pulpit as a living human being; the sacraments are the hard material facts of water, bread, and wine. While discussing the materiality of the Eucharist, Luther once remarked that we can chew the body of Christ with our teeth. Yet in themselves, these facts are simple phenomena: an anthology of writings collected over time by fallible human beings, perhaps an unimpressive preacher with little intellect and a nasty personality, cold water, stale bread, and sour wine. But grace in the form of the Holy Spirit reaches out to human beings so that we can find God's Word incarnated in these everyday phenomenal realties. Again, the mystics would not have quarreled with Luther in this regard.

So while Lutheran theology tends to induce skepticism about all attempts to attain religious certainty by means of literalist interpretations of the Bible or by the absolutism of church authority, it is equally suspicious about the alleged certainties of subjective religious experience, and rightly so. Absolutizing any experience leads to the sort of rigid fundamentalism that confuses belief in doctrines with faith. Again, mystics like Marguerite Porete, Meister Eckhart, John of the Cross, and others would have concurred. They would also be in agreement with the Lutheran tradition's rather sober view of the structure of Christian existence: human beings are fallen creatures, and the quest for perfection is as futile as it is illusionary. There are no Lutheran saints, but only human beings that are simultaneously "saint and sinner" (*simul iustus et peccator*). This soberness makes it extremely difficult to be a fundamentalist, which is not to say that there have not existed fundamentalist Lutherans.

But as far as I can tell, the mystics were not looking for perfection in Luther's meaning of this term. They certainly understood that human beings are sinful, and that whatever overcoming of egoism that occurs in practicing the mystical Way is the result of God's grace and not of the mystic's self-efforts to achieve a perfection that would please God. The mystics did not attempt to achieve union with God so much as to open their lives to the possibility that God's grace might replace the mystic's willfulness so that, again as Marguerite Porete explained it, a mystic might apprehend the universe as God apprehends the universe and love it accordingly.

But there are, of course, as Catherine Keller writes, "truths about everything":

> But in the vicinity of religion, and in particular of Christianity, truth has also served as a code for "God" and whatever God reveals. But even if we understand God to be "absolute"—nonbiblical but conventional language—that understanding does not make, or need not make, any human language (however inspired, however truthful, however revealed) absolute.[2]

---

2. Keller, *On the Mystery*, 4.

Still, the fear that has haunted Christian faith and practice for two thousand years is the relativity of all theological points of view and doctrinal interpretations. For nonmystics, mystics seem to take doctrines and definitions as metaphors rather than factual descriptions of God and Jesus as the Christ. They seem to many theologians to be relativists. Traditionally theologians are supposed to be the professionals, seeking doctrinal clarity about the incredible variety of Christian experiences, beliefs, and practices in order to establish the defining norms of what it means to be a Christian. It is certainly the case that Luther was forced to more systematically define the Lutheran part of the Reformation over against Calvinism, the Swiss Reformation, the enthusiasts, and the Roman Catholic Church. The Roman Catholic Church tried to counter the Protestant Reformation with its own Counter-Reformation. The search continues with as much intensity, but perhaps with less violence, as in past periods of Christian history for clear doctrinal norms defining what it means to be a Christian in the twenty-first-century world of religious and secular pluralism. Of course the challenges facing systematic theologians today are different from past challenges, but structurally the search for doctrinal continuity and certainty continues. The most notable exception is process theology's emphasis on the relativity ingredient in a religiously plural world.

As any good process theologian understands, the word *relativity* merely describes the relational universe that originates in Albert Einstein's special and general theories of relativity. All truth claims, including theological truth claims, are relative to context and perspective. But it does not follow that truth or value is *nothing but* that perspective. Furthermore, there have been theologians since Saint Paul who have resisted the temptation to identify any human perspective with divine revelation. Numerous theologians whose perspectives were sensitive to their own relativity have not uncritically slid toward a debilitating relativism of the sort that asserts all truth claims as equally true within their own perspectives and as equally false outside their perspectives. Included in this group of thinkers are the mystical theologians of the Christian Way.

Consequently, the lessons Christians need to learn from Christian mystics, as well as from theologians too numerous to list exhaustively—the list includes Augustine, Thomas Aquinas, Peter Abelard, Martin Luther, John Wesley, and contemporary theologians represented by Reinhold and H. Richard Niebuhr, Paul Tillich, and, yes, even Karl Barth, as well as process theologian John B. Cobb Jr.—is that what we call God is literally

LIVING WITHOUT A WHY: THE WAY OF GRACE

not God. These theologians all warn, each in his own distinctive ways, that theological reflection is constantly tempted to mistake the infinite for finite names and images—for the metaphors with which we clothe the infinite or the Sacred. So when we step away from the mystery that the mystics so systematically sought to step into, and when we make totalizing claims for Christian truths and beliefs, we in reality perpetuate antagonistic dualisms that paralyze rather than foster Christian faith. Relativity is thereby dissolved into indifferently debilitating relativism, and truth is frozen into deified absolutes.

The mystics of Christian tradition would have us avoid frozen truth and deified absolutes. In the words of Saint Augustine, "If you have understood, what is understood is not God."[3] Or as Meister Eckhart put it, "So be silent and do not chatter about God; for when you chatter about him, you are telling lies and sinning."[4] What we *call* God is literally not God. Theological reflection is perpetually tempted to mistake the infinite for the finite names and images in which we clothe it. Every religious tradition has its own mystical tradition, its own language of mystery, of unsaying, whose words put a check on its own particular idolatries—not by inhibiting their distinctive metaphors and narratives, but by critiquing their absolutisms. Mystics of every religious Way point out the cracks of their own particular idolatries. Mystics everywhere at all times and in all places negate, or as we say now, deconstruct, the absolutisms that presume to name the infinite as some person or entity, that claims to know God with any certainty, abstractly or literally. In Christian language, mystics keep theological reflection centered on the way of grace, the way of living without a why.

So when it comes down to it, Christian mystical theology and Martin Luther's own religious experience and theological reflection are neither conceptually nor experientially far apart at all. Nor are Marguerite Porete's experience of "living without a why," Luther's theology of grace, and contemporary process theology far apart. For we, and everything else caught in this space-tine universe, do not exist outside our relationships. We become who we are only in relation to a network of other creatures at all times and in all places. In such a universe, doing theology is not identical with faith. It is faith's quest for understanding, an understanding that is never final, complete, or reducible to doctrines "once and for all delivered to the saints."

---

3. Augustine, Sermon 52, 66, cited in Keller, *On the Mystery*, 18.

4. Sermon 83: *Renovamini spititu*, in Colledge and McGinn, *Meister Eckhart*, 207; also cited in Keller, *On the Mystery*, 18.

Propositional certainty renders religious faith redundant. The mystics of the Christian Way, from the historical Jesus to mystics like Marguerite Porete, teach us that if faith means believing in doctrines, then it shuts down the gospel. This is the error of Christian fundamentalism whenever and wherever it occurs. The only test for truth is pragmatic: if truth is what sets us free, we can only recognize truth by its liberating effects.

So what is the structure of existence of living without a why, of living by grace? The Way of the historical Jesus provides faithful Christians with a model. As noted in a previous chapter, Jesus spoke of two ways of living: a wise way and a foolish way, a way of life and a way of death, a narrow way and a broad way. The wise way is living without a why:

> Enter through the narrow gate; for the gate is wide and the road is easy that leads to destruction, and there are many who take it. For the gate is narrow and the road is hard that leads to life, and there are few who find it. (Matt 7:13–14)

For most conventionally religious and secular people, the wise way is the way of rules and regulations that successful people follow to meet the requirements for such achievements as attaining university degrees, earning tenure if one is an academic, achieving financial success, achieving social status, finding a spouse and raising a family, building a retirement portfolio, and, if one is Christian, attending church and living by Christian moral principles in order to demonstrate that one is worthy of redemption. In other words, a conventionally successful life is a life of fulfilling requirements that earn all sorts of stuff for one's life that we cannot take with us when we die. This is what Saint Paul had in mind with such phrases as "living by the works of the law" and "life according to the flesh," and what Luther had in mind by the word *works*.

The way of subversive wisdom, of living without a why, is quite different, although on the surface it might appear similar to the way the majority of human beings try to structure their lives. Mystics like Marguerite Porete earned their way in the world, did jobs that needing doing. They were active, but critical, participants in the communities of their time, including the institutional church. But they seem not to have had any desire to cling to achieving goals as a means of constructing self-gratifications; for such mystics, these had no permanence because there exists no permanent self to gratify. The task at hand was enough, without attachment to "the fruits of action"—as the *Bhagavad Gita* describes Karma Yoga—with no regard to achieving status either in society or before God. "Living without a why" is what Luther meant by grace pushed to its logical conclusion.

So the mystics took Jesus's image of God quite literally. For them, God is not a judge whose legal requirements must be met, not a legitimator of conventional wisdom, but gracious and compassionate. A favorite text that the mystics used for the discipline of *lectio divina* ("divine reading") and contemplation, also referred to in the previous chapter, is Matt 6:25–34:

> Therefore I tell you, do not worry about your life, what you will eat or what you will drink, or about your body, what you will wear. Is not life more than food, and the body more than clothing? Look at the birds of the air; they neither sow nor reap nor gather into barns, and yet their heavenly Father feeds them. Are you not of more value than they? And can any you by worrying add a single hour to your span of life? And why do you worry about clothing? Consider the lilies of the field, how they grow; they neither toil nor spin, yet I tell you, even Solomon in all his glory was not clothed as one of these. But if God so clothes the grass of he field, which is alive today and tomorrow is thrown into oven, will he not much more clothe you—you of little faith? Therefore, do not worry, saying, "What will we eat?" or "What will we drink?" or "What will we wear?" For it is the Gentiles who strive for all these things; indeed your heavenly Father knows that you need all these things. . . . .So do not worry about tomorrow, for tomorrow will bring worries of its own. Today's trouble is enough for today.

Marguerite Porete portrays a soul "ravished" by the grace of God's love and enabled to live without a why:

> The One in whom she is does His work through her, for the sake of which she is entirely freed by the witness of God Himself . . . who is the worker of this work to the profit of this soul who no longer has within her any work.[5]

Meister Eckhart has puts it this way:

> If anyone went on for a thousand years asking of life: "Why are you living?" life, if it could answer, would only say, "I live so that I may live." That is because life lives out of its own ground and springs from its own source, and so it lives without asking why it is itself living.[6]

---

5. Porete, *Mirror*, 121.
6. Sermon 5b, in Colledge and McGinn, *Meister Eckhart*, 184.

Martin Luther has the following:

> Only faith... extinguishes all wisdom of the flesh and all insistence on knowledge and makes one ready to be taught and led and willing to listen and to yield. For God does not require a magnitude of works but the mortification of the old [human being] in us. But [the old human being] cannot be mortified except by faith, which humbles our self-will and subjects it to that of another. For the life of the old [human being] is concentrated in the thinking or mind or wisdom and prudence of the flesh just as the life the serpent is centered in the head.[7]

And faith, according to Luther, is created in human beings by grace alone, which enables us to live, however imperfectly, in the words or Marguerite Porete, "without a why": that is, to live the Jesus way with no strings attached—at all. Even though the conceptualities and theological constructs employed by Marguerite Porete, Meister Eckhart, and Martin Luther are quite different, nevertheless the theologies of all three end up interpreting the structure of Christian existence engendered by the experience of grace as living without a why. It is the way of grace through faith alone. Everything else is peripheral.

---

7. "Lectures on Romans," in Pauck, *Lecture on Romans*, 290. I have inserted "human being" in place of "man" in this quotation since Luther was referring to both men and women.

Bibliography

Anslem, Saint. *Proslogium Monologium: An Appendix, in Behalf of the Fool*. Translated by S. N. Dean. Religion of Science Library 154. La Salle, IL: Open Court, 1954.
Armstrong, Karen. *The Case for God*. New York: Random House, 2009.
Augustine, Saint. *Confessions*. Translated with an introduction and notes by Henry Chadwick. World's Classics. Oxford: Oxford University Press, 1991.
———. *On Christian Doctrine*. Translated by D. W. Robertson. Library of Liberal Arts 80. Indianapolis: Bobbs-Merrill, 1958.
Bellah, Robert N. *Religion in Human Evolution: From the Paleolithic to the Axial Age*. Cambridge, MA: Belknap, 2011.
Bonhoeffer, Dietrich. *The Cost of Discipleship*. 2nd rev. ed. New York: Macmillan, 1959.
Borg, Marcus J. *The Heart of Christianity*. New York: HarperSanFrancisco, 2003.
———. *Meeting Jesus Again for the First Time*. New York: HarperSanFrancisco, 1994.
———. *Jesus: Uncovering the Life, Teachings, and Relevance of a Religious Revolutionary*. San Francisco: Harper One, 2006.
Brooke, John Hedley. *Science and Religion: Some Historical Perspectives*. Cambridge History of Science. Cambridge: Cambridge University Press, 1991.
Brunn, Emilie Zum, and Georgette Epiney-Burgard. *Women Mystics in Medieval Europe*. Translated by Sheila Hughes. New York: Paragon House, 1989.
Cobb, John B., Jr., and David Ray Griffin. *Process Theology: An Introductory Exposition*. Philadelphia: Westminster, 1976.
Colledge, Edmund, and Bernard McGinn, eds. and trans. *Meister Eckhart: The Essential Sermons, Commentaries, Treatises, and Defense*. Classics of Western Spirituality. New York: Paulist, 1981.
Craffert, Pieter F. *The Life of a Galilean Shaman: Jesus of Nazareth in Anthropological-Historical Perspective*. Matrix: The Bible in Mediterranean Context 3. Eugene, OR: Cascade Books, 2007.
Crossan, John Dominic. *The Birth of Christianity*. San Francisco: HarperSanFrancisco, 1998.
———. *The Historical Jesus: The Life of a Mediterranean Jewish Peasant*. San Francisco: HarperSanFrancisco, 1991.
———. *Jesus: A Revolutionary Biography*. San Francisco: HarperSanFrancisco. 1994.
D'Aquili, Eugene, and Andrew B. Newberg. *The Mystical Mind: Probing the Biology of Religious Experience*. Minneapolis: Fortress, 1999.
Dorrien, Gary J. *The Making of American Liberal Theology: Crisis, Irony, and Postmodernity 1950–2005*. Louisville: Westminster John Knox, 2006.

BIBLIOGRAPHY

Eliade, Mircea. *Shamanism: Archaic Techniques of Ecstasy.* Bollingen Series 76. Princeton: Princeton University Press, 1964.

Gallacher, Patrick J., ed. *The Cloud of Unknowing.* Middle English Texts. Kalamazoo, MI: Medieval Institute Publications, 1997.

Graham. A. C., trans. *Chuang Tzu: The Seven Inner Chapters and Other Writings from the Book Chuang-tzu.* London: Allen & Unwin, 1981.

Hall, David L. "On Seeking a Change in the Environment." In *Nature in Asian Traditions of Thought,* edited by J. Baird Callicott and Roger T. Ames. SUNY Series in Philosophy and Biology. Albany: State University of New York Press, 1989.

Hall, Douglas John. *What Christianity Is Not: An Exercise in "Negative" Theology.* Eugene, OR: Cascade Books, 2012.

Hamm, Berndt. *The Early Luther: Stages in a Reformation Reorientation.* Grand Rapids: Eerdmans, 2010.

Hanson, K. C. "How Honorable! How Shameful!: A Cultural Analysis of Matthew's Makarisms and Reproaches." *Semeia* 68 (1996) 83–114.

Hanson, K. C., and Douglas E. Oakman. *Palestine in the Time of Jesus: Social Structures and Social Conflicts.* Minneapolis: Fortress, 1998.

———. *Palestine in the Time of Jesus: Social Structures and Social Conflicts.* 2nd ed. Minneapolis: Fortress, 2008.

Hartshorne, Charles. *Divine Relativity: A Social Conception of God.* Terry Lectures. New Haven: Yale University Press, 1948.

———. *Omnipotence and Other Theological Mistakes.* Albany: State University of New York Press, 1984.

Hedrick, Charles W. *The Wisdom of Jesus: Between the Sages of Israel and the Apostles of the Church.* Eugene, OR: Cascade Books, 2014.

Hollywood, Amy. *The Soul as Virgin Wife.* Notre Dame, IN: University of Notre Dame Press, 1995.

———. "Suffering Transformed: Marguerite Porete, Meister Eckhart, and the Problem of Women's Spirituality," In *Meister Eckhart and the Beguine Mystics,* edited by Bernard McGinn, 87–113. New York: Continuum, 1994.

Idel, Moshe, and Bernard McGinn, eds. *Mystical Union in Judaism, Christianity, and Islam: An Ecumenical Dialogue.* New York: Continuum: 1990.

Ingram, Paul O. *Buddhist-Christian Dialogue in an Age of Science.* Lanham, MD: Rowman & Littlefield, 2008.

———. *The Dharma of Faith: An Introduction to Classical Pure Land Buddhism.* Washington DC: University Press of America, 1977.

———. *The Modern Buddhist-Christian Dialogue: Two Universalistic Religions of Transformation.* Studies in Comparative Religions 2. Lewiston, NY: Mellen, 1988.

———. *Theological Reflections at the Boundaries.* Eugene, OR: Cascade Books, 2012.

———. *Wrestling with God.* Eugene, OR: Cascade Books, 2006.

———. *Wrestling with the Ox: A Theology of Religious Experience.* 1997. Reprinted, Eugene, OR: Wipf & Stock, 2006.

Johnston. William. *Silent Music: The Science of Meditation.* New York: Harper & Row, 1974.

Katz, Steven T. "Language, Epistemology, and Mysticism." In *Mysticism and Philosophical Analysis,* edited by Steven T. Katz, 22–74. New York: Oxford University Press, 1978.

Keller, Catherine. *On the Mystery: Discerning Divinity in Process.* Minneapolis: Fortress, 2008.

BIBLIOGRAPHY

Kim, hee-Jin. *Dōgen Kigen: Mystical Realist.* Monographs of the Association for Asian Studies 29. Tucson: University of Arizona Press, 1975.

Kitagawa Joseph M. "Primitive, Classical, and Modern Religions: A Perspective on Understanding History of Religions." In *The History of Religions: Essays in the Problem of Understanding*, edited by Jerold C. Brauer, 39–54. Essay in Divinity 1. Chicago: University of Chicago Press, 1967.

Lichtmann, Matia. "Marguerite Porete and Meister Eckhart: The Mirror of Simple Souls Mirrored." In *The Flowering of Mysticism: Men and Women in the New Mysticism—1200-1350*, edited by Bernard McGinn, 65–86. The Presence of God 3. New York: Crossroad, 1998.

Luther, Martin. *Freedom of a Christian.* In *Martin Luther: Selections from His Writings*, edited by John Dillenberger, 60–61. Anchor Books. New York: Doubleday, 1962.

Masunaga, Reiho. *A Primer of Sōtō Zen: A Translation of Dōgen's Shōbōgenzō Zuimonki.* East-West Center Book. Honolulu: University Press of Hawaii, 1971.

McNamara, Joanne. "The Rhetoric of Orthodoxy: Clerical Authority and Female Innovation in the Struggle with Heresy." In *Maps of Flesh and Light: The Religious Experience of Medieval Women Mystics*, edited by Ullrike Wiethaus, 9–27. Syracuse, NY: Syracuse University Press, 1993.

McGinn, Bernard, ed. *The Flowering of Mysticism: Men and Women in the New Mysticism (1200-1350).* The Presence of God 3. New York: Crossroad, 1998.

———, ed. *Foundations of Mysticism.* The Presence of God 1. New York: Crossroad, 1992.

———. "Meister Eckhart and the Beguines in the Contest of Vernacular Theology." In *Meister Eckhart and the Beguine Mystics: Hadewijch of Brabant, Mechthild of Magdeburg, and Marguerite Porete*, edited by Bernard McGinn, 1–14. New York: Continuum, 1994.

———, ed. *Meister Eckhart and the Beguine Mystics: Hadewijch of Brabant, Mechthild of Magdeburg, and Marguerite Porete.* New York: Continuum, 1994.

Merton, Thomas. *Contemplative Prayer.* New York: Image Books, 1990.

———. *Entering the Silence: Becoming a Monk & Writer.* Edited by Jonathan Montaldo. The Journals of Thomas Merton 2. San Francisco: Harper, 1996.

———. "Monastic Experience and East-West Dialogue." In *The Asian Journals of Thomas Merton*, edited by Naomi Burton Stone et al., 309–17. New York: New Directions, 1975.

———. *Zen and the Birds of Appetite.* New York: New Directions, 1968.

Midgley, Mary. "Concluding Reflections: Dover Beach Revisited." In *The Oxford Handbook of Religion and Science*, edited by Philip Clayton and Zachary Simpson, 962–77. Oxford Handbooks. Oxford: Oxford University Press, 2006.

Mitchell, Donald W., and James Wiseman, eds. *The Gethsemani Encounter: A Dialogue on the Spiritual Life by Buddhist and Christian Monastics.* New York: Continuum, 1998.

Mommaers, Paul, and Jan van Bragt. *Mysticism, Buddhist and Christian.* New York: Crossroad, 1995.

Niebuhr, H. Richard. *Radical Monotheism and Western Culture: With Supplementary Essays.* Library of Theological Ethics. Louisville: Westminster John Knox, 1993.

Nishitani, Keiji. *Religion and Nothingness.* Translated by Jan van Bragt. 1969. Nanzan Studies in Religion and Culture. Berkeley: University of California Press, 1982.

Nygren, Anders. *Agape and Eros.* Translated by Philip S. Watson. Philadelphia: Westminster, 1953.

Oakman, Douglas E. *Jesus and the Peasants.* Matrix 4. Eugene, OR: Cascade Books, 2008.

BIBLIOGRAPHY

———. *Jesus, Debt, and the Lord's Prayer.* Eugene, OR: Cascade Books, 2014.

———. "The Perennial Relevance of Saint Paul: Paul's Understanding of Christ and a Time of Radical Pluralism." *Biblical Theology Bulletin* 39 (2009) 4–14.

———. *The Political Aims of Jesus.* Minneapolis: Fortress, 2012.

Pauck, Wilhelm, trans. and ed. *Lecture on Romans*, by Martin Luther. Library of Christian Classics 15. Philadelphia: Westminster, 1961.

Peterson, Gregory R. *Minding God: Theology and the Cognitive Sciences.* Theology and the Sciences. Minneapolis: Fortress, 2003.

Polkinghorne, John. *Belief in God in an Age of Science.* Terry Lectures. New Haven: Yale University Press, 1998.

Porete, Marguerite. *The Mirror of Simple Souls.* Translated and introduced by Ellen L. Babinsky. The Classics of Western Spirituality. New York: Paulist, 1993

Sells, Michael A. *The Mystical Languages of Unsaying.* Chicago: University of Chicago Press, 1994.

———. "The Pseudo-Woman and the Meister: 'Unsaying' and Essentialism." In *Meister Eckhart and the Beguine Mystics: Hadewijch of Brabant, Mechthild of Magdeburg, and Marguerite Porete*, edited by Bernard McGinn, 114–46. New York: Continuum, 1994.

Shreeve, James. "Beyond the Brain." *National Geographic Magazine* 207/3 (March 2005) 2–31. Online: http://science.nationalgeographic.com/science/health-and-human-body/human-body/mind-brain/.

Smith, Barbara Herrnstein. *Scandalous Knowledge: Science Truth, and the Human.* Science and Cultural Theory. Durham: Duke University Press, 2006.

Smith Wilfred Cantwell. *Belief and History.* Richard Lectures for 1974–75, University of Virginia. Charlottesville: University Press of Virginia, 1977.

———. *Faith and Belief.* Princeton: Princeton University Press, 1979.

———. *The Faith of Other Men.* New York: New American Library, 1963.

———. *The Meaning and End of Religion.* Minneapolis: Fortress, 1991.

Suzuki, D. T. "Satori." In *The Essentials of Zen Buddhism: An Anthology of the Writings of Daisetz T. Suzuki*, edited by Barnard Phillips, 201–16. New York: Dutton, 1962.

Wach, Joachim. *Sociology of Religion.* Chicago: University of Chicago Press, 1964.

Waley, Arthur, trans. *The Way and Its Power: A Study of the Tao Te Ching and Its Place in Chinese Thought.* UNESCO Collection of Representative Works. Chinese Works. New York: Grove Press, 1958.

Wallace B. Alan. *Hidden Dimensions: The Unification of Physics and Consciousness.* The Columbia Series in Science and Religion. New York: Columbia University Press, 2007.

Watson, Burton, trans. *The Complete Works of Chuang Tzu.* UNESCO Collection of Representative Works. Chinese Works. New York: Columbia University Press, 1968.

Whitehead, Alfred N. *Modes of Thought.* New York: Macmillan, 1938.

———. *Process and Reality: An Essay in Cosmology.* Edited by David Ray Griffin and Donald W. Sherburne. Gifford Lectures 1927/28. Corrected ed. New York: Free Press, 1985.

———. *Science and the Modern World.* Lowell Institute Lectures, 1925. New York: Macmillan, 1926.

Index of Scriptures

OLD TESTAMENT

Genesis
32:24–31	31

Deuteronomy
34:10	93

NEW TESTAMENT

Matthew
5:14	96n
6:5–14	107
6:25–34	115
6:24	96n
6:25	98
6:26–29	99
6:30	99
7:13–14	98
7:16	96n
8:22	96n
10:38	101n
13:33	96
13:44	96
21:1–10	98
23:24	96n
28	104

Mark
1:10	94
8:34	101n
9:33–40	1
9:33–37	1
9:38–40	3
14:32–42	108

Luke
6:39	96n
6:44	96n
9:60	96n
12:24–27	99
12:28	99
13:20	96
14:16–24	98
14:26	98
14:27	101n
15:11–32	100n
16:13	96n
19:13	98
24:13–35	104
24:36–49	104

John
1:1–18	37, 108

Acts
9:3–9	93

INDEX OF SCRIPTURES

2 Corinthians

12:1–4   93

1 John 4:8   62n

BUDDHIST SCRIPTURES

Lotus Sutra   47

DAOIST SCRIPTURES

Dao De Ching   67–69

Zuangzi   7, 67–73, 79

HINDU SCRIPTURES

Bhagavad Gita   114

Upanishads   26, 52

ISLAMIC SCRIPTURES & WRITINGS

Hadith   35

Qur'an   5, 26, 35, 51, 53, 55, 56, 80, 90, 107n

Index of Names

Abelard, Peter, 44–45, 112
Abraham, 92
Amidah Buddha, *see* Buddha
Anslem, Saint, 38, 46
Apalatin, Georg, 109
Aquinas, Thomas, *see* Thomas Aquinas
Aristotle, 38, 106
Armstrong, Karen, 33
Augustine, Saint, 37, 58, 103, 109, 112, 113

Bellah, Robert N., 14
Bohr, Neils, 29
Bonhoeffer, Dietrich, 100
Borg, Marcus J., 7–8, 35, 76, 91, 93, 99, 100
Bragt, Jan van, 80
Brooke, John Hedley, 34
Brunn, Emilie Zum, 61
Buddha, 14, 16, 18, 21, 34, 35, 82, 90, 95, 105

Calvin, John, 40
Cobb, John B., Jr., xii, 38, 107, 112, 117
Colledge, Edmund, 113, 115, 117
Confucius, 95
Craffert, Pieter F., 8, 59, 91, 117
Crossan, John Dominic, 35, 93, 97, 117

D'Aquili, Eugene, 85–86, 117
Davidson, Richard, 83
Dickinson, Emily, 14

Eckhart, Meister, xi, 62, 79, 82, 111, 113, 115–16
Einstein, Albert, 14, 29, 112
Eliade, Mircea, 8, 11, 16, 17, 24, 91, 118
Epiney-Burgard, Georgette, 61

Gallacher, Patrick J., 90, 118
Gandhi, Mohatma, 5, 45, 91
Graham, A. C., 57, 118
Griffin, David Ray, 38, 107, 117, 120

Hall, David L., 118
Hall, Douglas John, 32, 118
Hanina ben Dosa, 93
Hanson, K. C., xii, 35, 97, 101, 118
Hartshorne, Charles, 20, 39, 40, 118
Hedrick, Charles W., 96, 118
Heisenberg, Werner, 29
Hollywood, Amy, 62, 63, 118
Honi the Circle-Drawer, 93

Idel, Moshe, 73, 118
Ingram, Paul O., vii–x, 1, 14, 19, 22, 23, 37, 53, 55, 56, 83, 118

Jesus, viii, xi, 1–5, 8, 26, 27, 33, 35–38, 41, 43–45, 49, 53–55, 76, 90–108, 110, 112, 114–16
Johanan ben Zakkai, 93
John the disciple, 3
John of the Cross, 8, 79, 91, 111
John the Baptist, 36
Johnston, William, 87

INDEX OF NAMES

Katz, Steven T., 84, 118
Keats, John, 14
Keller, Catherine,
Khan, Badhsha, 5
Kim, Hee-Jin, 82, 119
King, Martin Luther, Jr., 5, 45, 91
Kitagawa Joseph M., 11, 12, 17, 24, 119

Laozi, 67
Lichtmann, Matia, 62, 119
Luther, Martin, viii, xi, 8, 37, 40, 46, 51, 52, 54, 66, 103, 109–16, 119

Mark, 1–5
Masunaga, Reiho, 82, 119
McGinn, Bernard, 59, 62, 73, 113, 115, 117, 118, 119, 120
McNamara, Joanne, 119
Merton, Thomas, 30, 48, 81–82, 119
Midgley, Mary, 29, 119
Mitchell, Donald W., 81, 119
Mohammed, 35, 90, 91, 105, 107
Mommaers, Paul, 80, 119
Moriya Sensei, 48
Moses, 8, 26, 53, 91, 92, 93
Müller, Max, 11
Murray, Cecil, 5
Myōkō, Naganuma, 49

Newberg, Andrew B., 85–86, 117
Nichiren, 49
Niebuhr, H. Richard, 112, 119
Niebuhr, Reinhold, 105
Nikkyō, Niwano, 49
Nishitani, Keiji, 82, 119
Nygren, Anders, 39, 119

Oakman, Douglas E., xi, xii, 35, 91, 100, 101, 118, 119
Otto, Rudolf, 11, 16

Pauck, Wilhelm, 116, 120
Paul (Saul of Tarsus), Saint, xii, 30, 33, 37, 42–43, 93, 103–4, 112, 114

Peter, Saint, 1–2
Peterson, Gregory, 84, 120
Polkinghorne, John, 34, 120
Porete, Marguarite, viii, xi, 1, 5, 7–8, 30–31, 49, 57–58, 61–67, 72–73, 75, 79, 91, 100, 109–11, 113–16, 120

Romero, Oscar, 45

Sankara, 105
Santayana, George, 41
Sells, Michael, 57, 60–61, 62, 64, 65, 78, 120
Shizuteru, Ueda, 82
Shreeve, James, 83, 120
Sivaraksa, Sulak, 5
Smith, Barbara Herrnstein, 19, 120
Smith, Huston, 11
Smith Wilfred Cantwell, 11, 13, 14, 34, 120
Stephen I, 89
Stone, Naomi Barton, 119
Suzuki, D. T., 82, 120

Tanaka, 48–49
Tauler, Johnanes, 109
Thich Nhat Hanh, 91
Thomas Aquinas, 38–39, 112
Tillich, Paul, 34, 79, 90, 112

Ueda Roshi, 48–49, 82
Unno, Mark, 50

Wach, Joachim, 11
Waley, Arthur, 68–69, 120
Wallace, B. Alan, 85, 120
Watson, Burton, 57, 68–69, 72, 120
Weber, Max, 11
Wesley, John, 103, 112
Whitehead, Alfred N., vii, xii, 6, 15, 20, 23–27, 31, 40–41, 44–45, 52–56, 89, 106–7, 120
Wiseman, James, 81, 119

Zuangzi, viii, 7, 57–58, 61, 67–73